ADO
PHOTOSHOP
ELEMENT 2024

Handbook

A Comprehensive Handbook for Photographers and Artists from a Beginner to an Expert

LYON MUSK

TABLE OF CONTENTS

INTRODUCTION

What is Adobe Photoshop Elements 2024?

Adobe Photoshop Elements is a simple picture editing program. Go from simple picture adjustments to complete makeovers. AI, automation, and a modernized appearance simplify picture editing. No subscription is necessary.

What's New in Adobe Photoshop Elements 2024?

- **Match Color & Tone:** After selecting a color or tone, you may adjust the hue, saturation, and brightness by using an included preset or your photo.
- **Make and Share Picture Reels:** Create and save picture reels with your best images, each with a unique caption, effect, etc., to share on social media as MP4s or GIFs.
- **New User Interface:** Better fonts, icons, buttons, and colors are included, along with a choice between bright and dark modes.

- **One-Click Sky/Background Selection:** Improve or replace a portion of your shot with ease thanks to automatic selections.
- **One-Click Photo Quick Actions:** You can now quickly locate one-click adjustments from a single location.
- Eliminate JPEG Artifacts to provide compressed JPEGs a more realistic, smooth appearance.
- **Guided Edits:** To bring the total to 62, two additional guided edits, Photo Text and Replace Background, have been added.
- **Free Adobe Stock Photos:** Get free access to thousands of images.
- To create an effect influenced by artists and art movements, select Artistic Effects.

New light and dark Modes

Experience editing in a modern, fresh way with eye-pleasing fonts, icons, buttons, and colors. You can also select between light and dark mode settings. Modernized workspaces (Advanced, Guided, and Quick), dialog boxes, buttons, panels, toolbars, action bars, and more are all visible. The application's UI color mode can be adjusted to either light or dark from the options.

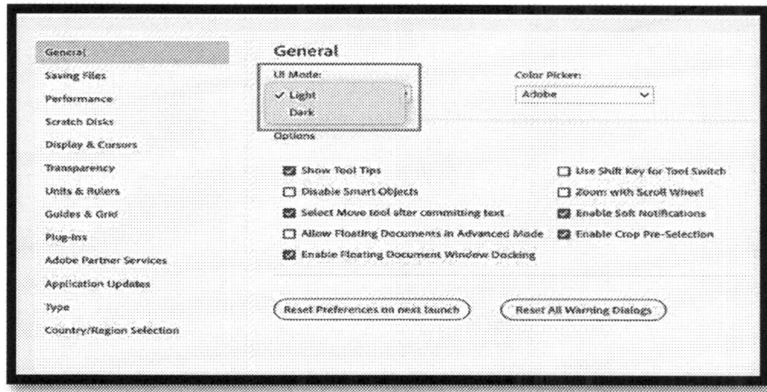

Color Match

Adjust the hue, saturation, and brightness after clicking once, or use one of the presets that are already included. Investigate the Quick and Advanced modes of the recently added Color Match function.

- Using the built-in settings in the Quick mode, adjust the color, saturation, and brightness.

- In the Advanced mode, in addition to the pre-installed presets, you can also utilize a picture of yourself as a custom preset and adjust the output's attributes.

Photo Reel

Favorite shots are quickly shown in reels, each with unique text, effects, and visuals. To facilitate sharing, save them as GIFs or MP4s.

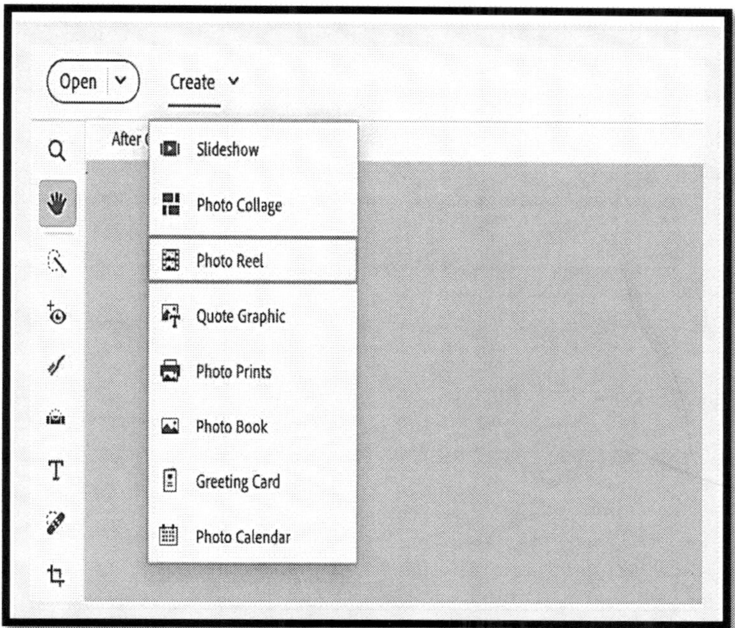

Add Text Guided Edit

All of the text options have been combined into a simple guided edit for this edition. Text can be aligned vertically, horizontally, or on a route or shape. Use patterns and gradients to warp and style it.

To make use of this guided edit tool, take these steps:

- Toggle between the Guided and preferred photo modes.
- To start the procedure, navigate to the Basics category and choose the Add Text guided edit card.
- Adhere to the instructions for editing.

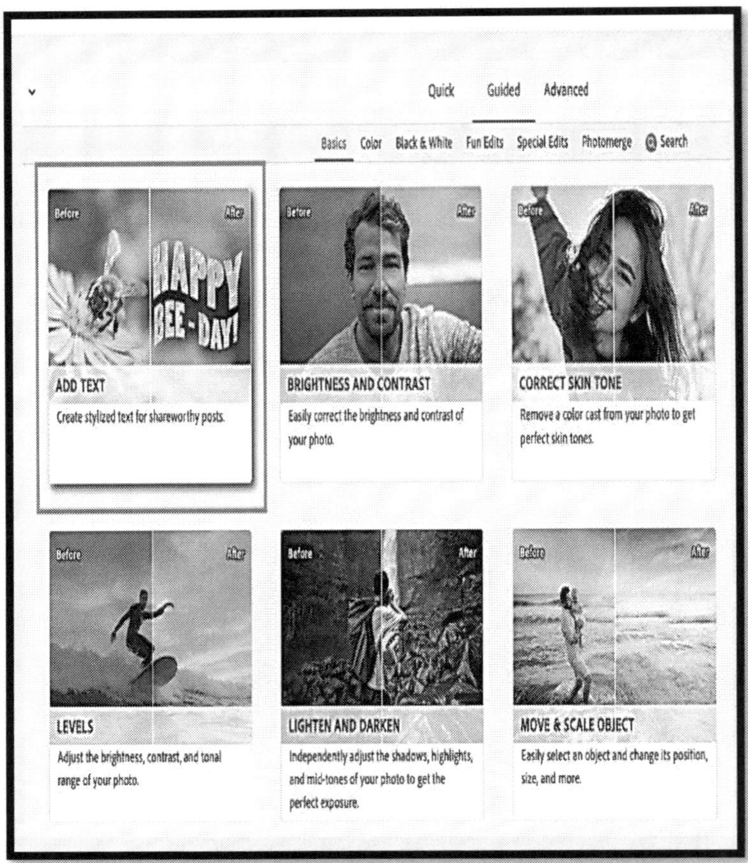

Quick Actions

Here are 25 of the most widely used one-click modifications that you can access instantly. With just one handy panel, you can instantly blur or eliminate a background, smooth skin, colorize a photo, and much more. When in Quick mode, the Quick Actions panel is adjacent to Effects.

The most well-liked one-click adjustments in Quick Actions - JPEG Artifacts Removal are listed below.

Automatic Smart Fix: Eliminate Background, Choose Subject, Smooth Skin

Free Images from Adobe Stock

Get free images from Adobe Stock to increase your creative potential. Use Photoshop Elements to create an inspirational Quote Graphic, experiment with different backgrounds, or collages with thousands of gorgeous stock photographs.

Using Adobe Stock, get free photos and backgrounds for these four Photoshop workflows:

File > Search > Graphics > Background Guided > Adobe Stock Expert mode Change the Background, Create > Quote graphic

New Artistic Effect

The new Artistic Effect options let you turn images into works of art. To add effects influenced by famous works of art or popular art genres, simply click. Powered by Sensei from Adobe.

One –Click the selection

Simply click to select a background or sky to make editing easier. Changing or improving a single area is made easy with automatic options, with power from Adobe Sensei.

There are two methods to make use of these one-click choose choices:

- Select Sky, Background, or Subject from the choices under the Select menu.

- Choose any option from Subject, Sky, or Background that is available within the action bar by opening any of the Selection Tools from the Tools panel.

Photoshop Elements Mobile and Web Companion Apps (English only Beta)

Mobile

One of the tools included in the licensed editions of Photoshop Elements 2024 is the Adobe Elements Mobile Companion App for 2024. The goal of this English-only beta software is to improve user experience by enabling a smooth transition between desktop apps and mobile devices.

The following are some of the upgrades and features

- Store images and movies in the cloud for convenient viewing and editing via desktop and browser applications.
- Basic editing tools for photos, including aspect ratio changes, rotation, cropping, and transformation.
- Photos may be instantly processed with one click using Quick Actions like as Auto Crop, Auto Straighten, Auto Tone, Auto White Balance, and Remove Background.
- When there isn't an internet connection, you may view and share media offline.
- 2GB of free cloud storage is available for pictures and movies.
- Bring in media from several sources on your phone.
- Multiple bug fixes, coupled with enhancements to UX and usability.
- Supports iOS 14.5 and Android versions 9 and above.

How to install the Android beta app

The procedures below can be used to install the Photoshop Elements 2024 Android beta app:

- Make sure your Android device is running on version 9 or higher.
- Open the Google Play Store using an Android smartphone.

- Find the Adobe Elements (Beta) application.
- To download and install the app on your smartphone, locate it and touch the Install button.
- Launch the application after installation, then log in using your Adobe ID.
- The beta capabilities ought to be available to you if you're a licensed user of Photoshop Elements 2024 or Premiere Elements 2024.
- If you've never used the app before, you may benefit from Adobe's 30-day free trial.

How to install the iOS beta app

Installing the Photoshop Elements 2024 iOS beta app is a simple procedure. Here's how to accomplish it:

- Verify that the iOS version on your smartphone is 14.5 or above.
- On your iOS device, install TestFlight from the Software Store. This is Apple's beta software download platform.

- Install the beta app via TestFlight by accepting your email invitation or by clicking on the public link invitation.
- After installing TestFlight, click the invitation link to launch the English-only beta of the Adobe Elements Mobile Companion App.
- Follow the instructions to install the beta app on your device.
- To use the features, open the application after it has been installed and log in using your Adobe ID.

Web

What the Adobe Elements online (web) beta application allows you to accomplish

- View, access, edit, and distribute images and videos
- The Media tab allows you to see, share, and access all of the images and movies that you have saved in the cloud. Click on any image or video to see it in full screen.

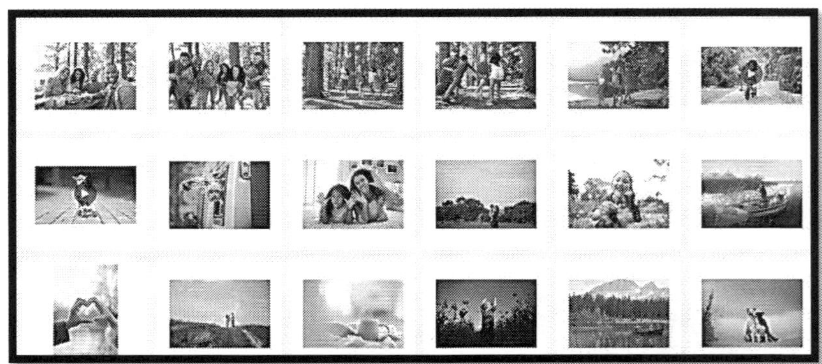

Click Share or Delete after selecting any photo or video to share or remove it.

Using the full-screen mode choices, you may also remove, download, or share certain images and movies.

Create and personalize slideshows and collages.

Cloud-stored images and videos may be used to make slideshows and picture collages. To start, go to the Creations screen and choose the Photo collage card or Slideshow option.

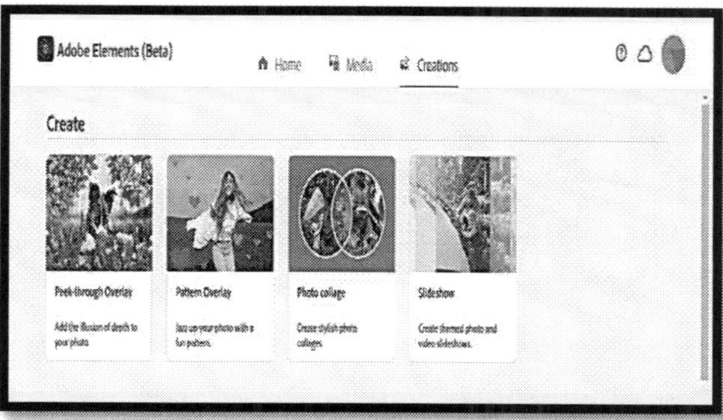

By selecting the required media and then clicking the build button in the action bar, you can easily build a Slideshow or Photo collage straight from the Media screen.

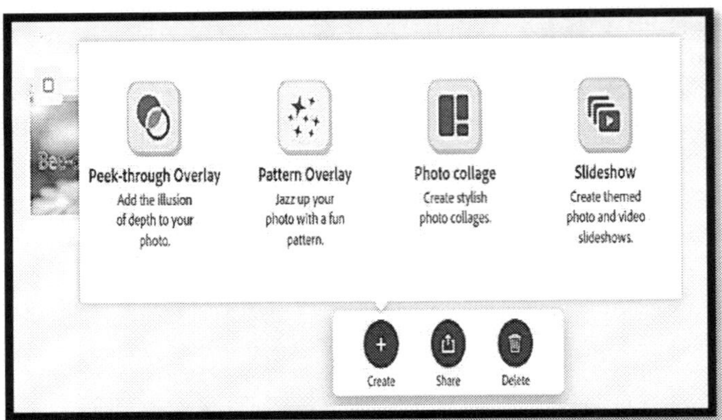

Once a slideshow has been generated, you may alter it by adjusting the Audio, adding or deleting Media, experimenting with different Templates, and adding a Title Slide.

Any picture collage may be made unique by adjusting the Layout, altering the Background, and adding or deleting Media.

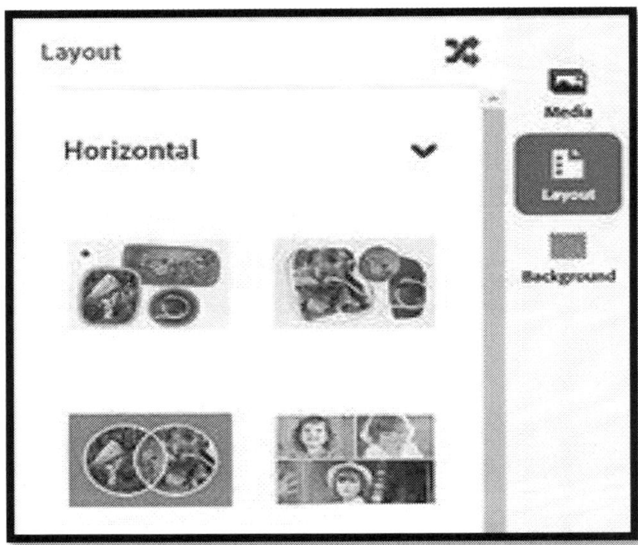

CHAPTER ONE

DISCOVERING POWER OF PHOTOSHOP ELEMENTS 2024

The Adobe Photoshop Element 2024 System Requirement for MAC and WINDOWS

WINDOWS

Microsoft Windows 10 (version 22H2) or Windows 11 (version 22H2), 64-bit versions only; Windows 7 and Windows 8.1 not supported; Intel 6th Generation or later CPU or AMD equivalent with SSE4.1 support
Eight gigabytes of RAM.
9 GB of accessible hard disk space is needed to install the application; extra space is needed for temporary files during product installation and use, and for downloading material from the internet (the application cannot be installed on removable flash storage devices or volumes that employ case-sensitive file systems).
Display resolution of 1280 x 800 (at 100% scale factor)
Windows Media Player is necessary for importing Windows Media files and is a sound and display driver compatible with Microsoft DirectX 12.

MACOS

Apple silicon M1 or newer CPU; Intel 6th Generation or newer processor; macOS 12, macOS 13 (13.4 or later)
Eight gigabytes of RAM
10 GB of accessible hard disk space is needed to install the application; extra space is needed for temporary files during product installation

and use, and for downloading material from the internet (the product cannot be installed on removable flash storage devices or volumes that employ case-sensitive file systems).
Display resolution of 1280 x 800 (at 100% scale factor)

For both Windows and macOS

Internet access is necessary for both Windows and macOS to activate products and download online content. Suggested specifications:

- Processors with AMD equivalents or Intel 7th Generation or above that enable SSE4.1 and AVX
- RAM of 16 GB for HD media
- For 4K media, 32 GB or more of RAM is required.
- A GPU with 4 GB RAM
- Quick internal SSD for caching and installing apps
- Extra fast drive (or drives) for media

Downloading and installing the Adobe Photoshop Element 2024

From the Adobe website, download and install

Make sure you have administrator access to the account you're using before you start, use the most recent version of Firefox, Chrome, Safari, or Internet Explorer. Verify that the Adobe ID you have is active. In your web browser, disable pop-up blockers. Turn off antivirus programs, firewalls, and third-party security software temporarily. The installation procedure is accelerated by disabling them, and verifying that the serial number you have for Photoshop Elements is active. To ensure that the installation is finished, make sure you are online.

Acquire Photoshop Elements

- Launch your web browser and navigate to the Adobe Photoshop Elements download page.
- Using your Adobe ID, log in. You can create an Adobe ID if you don't already have one.
- Choose the download language and platform.
- Click on Download.

Set up Photoshop Elements.

After downloading the installation file for Adobe Photoshop Elements from the Adobe website, open it, using your password and Adobe ID—typically your email address—to log in. On the subsequent screen that displays, choose Proceed. Follow these steps on the Installation Options screen, then click Continue: Choose a language and indicate the installation location.

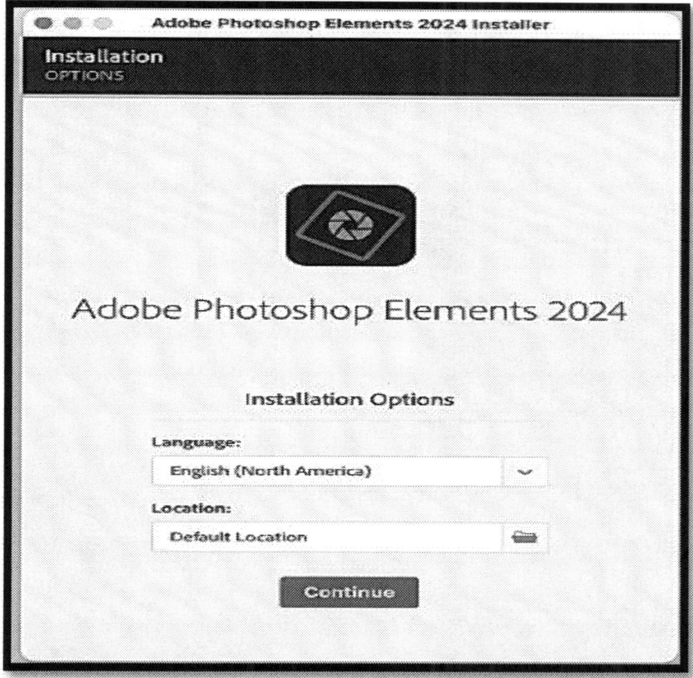

When the installation is running, you can see what's new in Photoshop Elements 2024 by clicking on the picture display that shows up at the bottom of the installer.

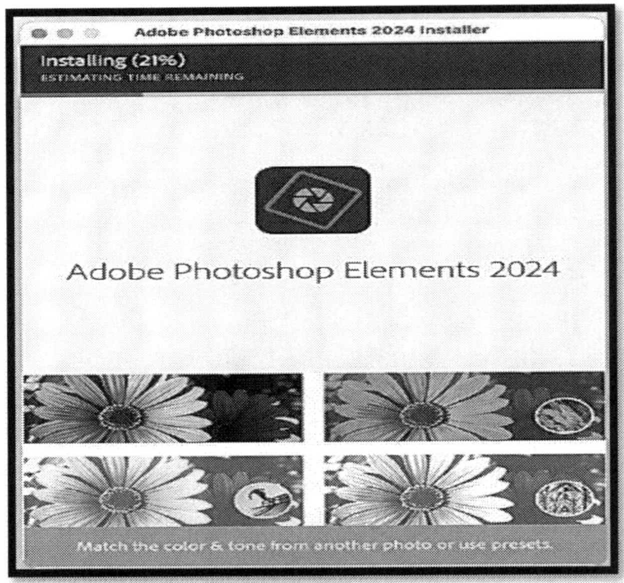

Choose Picture Editor from the screen that displays.

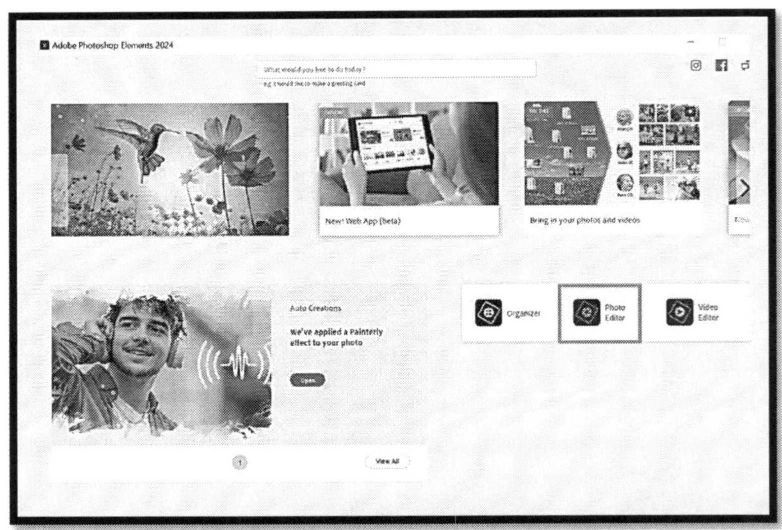

Enter your email address and password to sign in.

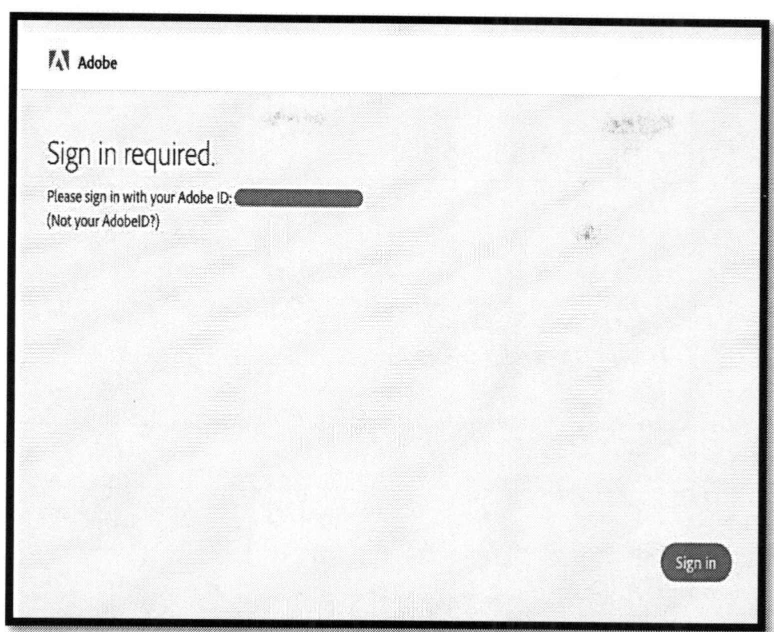

Choose Activate immediately On the Welcome screen.

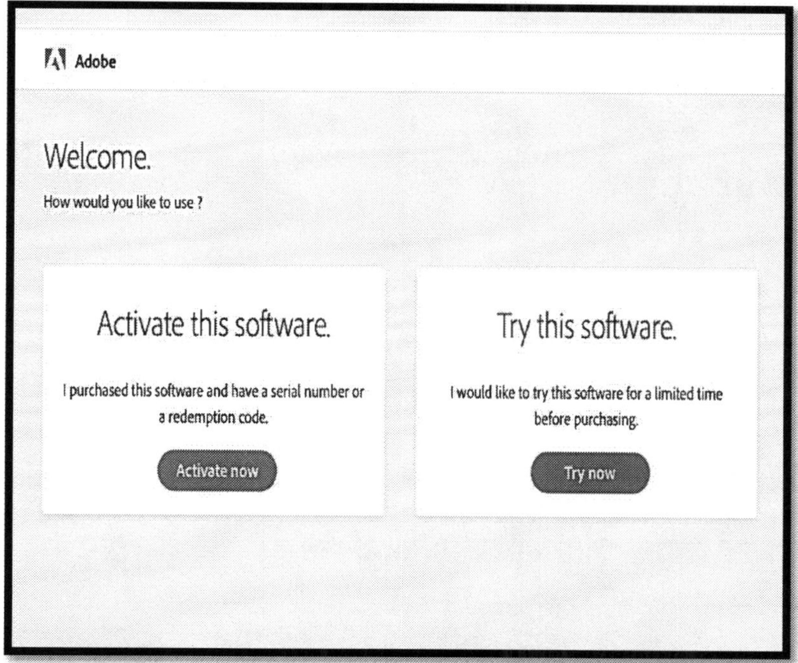

Select next after entering the serial number on the upcoming screen.

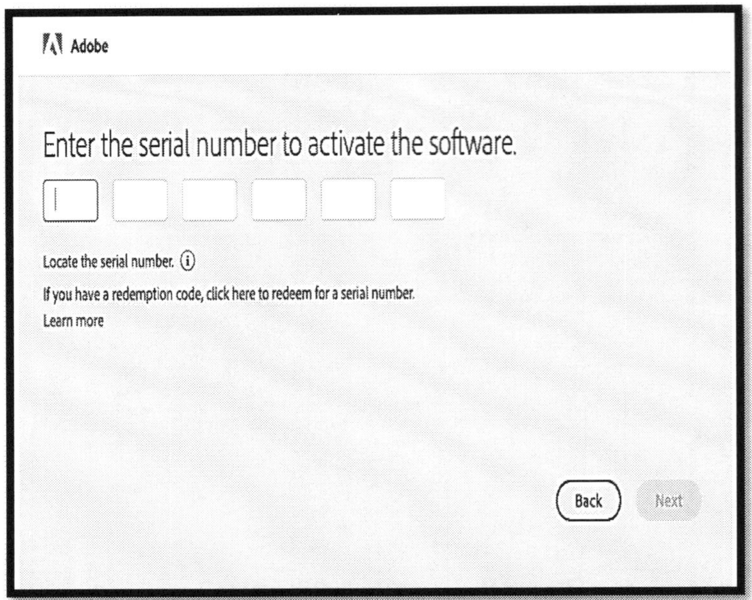

THINGS YOU OUGHT TO KNOW ABOUT PHOTOSHOP ELEMENT 2024

COLORS

About color

One of the main features of digital photographs is color. A variety of color models, including HSB and RGB, are available in Photoshop Elements 2024 and are necessary for color repair and modification.

HSB Model

The HSB (Hue, Saturation, Brightness) model allows you to adjust the hue to change the color, saturation to modify the intensity, and brightness to control the lightness or darkness of the color.

RGB Model

The RGB (Red, Green, Blue) model is based on the primary colors of light. This model is used for digital displays, cameras, and scanners. Photoshop Elements allows you to adjust these colors to achieve the desired effect.

Color Wheel

The color wheel is a visual representation of colors arranged according to their chromatic relationship. It's a useful tool for selecting harmonious colors and creating color schemes in your designs.

The Photo Bin

The Photo Bin in Photoshop Elements is a convenient area at the bottom of the workspace that displays thumbnails of open files. It makes it easy to switch between images while editing.

Image Size and Canvas Size

Image Size refers to the dimensions of your image in pixels and is crucial for the resolution and quality of your image.
Canvas Size is the total area available for an image. Adjusting the canvas size can add or remove space around the image without altering the image itself.

Selections

These are areas of a photo that you define and can edit. Photoshop Elements 2024 offers one-click selections for subjects, skies, or backgrounds using Adobe Sensei AI technology

Layers

The term "layers" refers to a stack of translucent sheets that allow you to work on distinct areas of your image independently of one another without impacting the others.

Alpha Channels

These store selections as editable grayscale masks in the Channels panel, allowing you to isolate and protect areas of an image as you apply edits

RASTER AND VECTOR GRAPHICS

Raster

Images are made up of pixels, which can lose quality when scaled up. Photoshop Elements handles raster images with tools to edit and enhance them

Vector

These may be resized without sacrificing quality because they are composed of paths, as opposed to rasters. Though it might not be as capable as Adobe Illustrator when it comes to vector work, Photoshop Elements can handle most vector elements.

Pixels

A raster image is composed of tiny dots known as pixels. Resolution increases with the number of pixels in an image.

Megapixel

One megapixel equals one million pixels. It's a term often used to describe the resolution of digital cameras.

PPI and DPI

A digital image's resolution is measured in pixels per inch (PPI), whereas a printed image's resolution is measured in dots per inch (DPI). Finer detail is indicated by higher values.

Resolution

This indicates how much detail is contained in an image. More image detail corresponds with higher resolution. A higher DPI is recommended for printing to guarantee high-quality results.

CHAPTER TWO

EXPLORING THE EXCITING FEATURES IN ADOBE PHOTOSHOP ELEMENTS 2024

Completely Revised user interface (UI)

The user interface (UI) of Adobe Photoshop Elements 2024 has been fully redesigned, giving the program a modern aesthetic and enhanced features. The following are a few noteworthy changes:

Dark Mode: To change the background from the default white to a darker one, a new dark mode option has been added. This can make long editing sessions easier on the eyes and aid in visually offsetting images.

Redesigned Menus and Fonts: The user interface (UI) has been redesigned with new buttons, colors, icons, and fonts to give a more streamlined and contemporary experience.

Efficient Access to One-Click Fixes: Quick action panels have been consolidated, making it easier to access various editing options. These are organized into categories like Background, Subject, and Creative, with 25 options including new features such as Select Background, Select Sky, and Remove JPEG Artifacts.

Guided Edits: The software continues to offer helpful step-by-step guided edits, which are a great resource for learning new skills.

Color Match: A new feature called Color Match allows users to transfer or simulate the color tone of one image to another, which can be useful for creating a unified look across a series of photos.

Discover one –click Quick Actions all in one Place

The following easy instructions will show you where to find one-click Quick Actions in Adobe Photoshop Elements 2024:

- Get your image loaded by opening Adobe Photoshop Elements.
- Navigate to Quick mode and select the Quick Actions panel, which is beside Effects.
- Popular single-click adjustments are available to you here, speeding up and streamlining photo editing.
- You may quickly colorize, smooth skin, blur, or erase the background from a shot, among other things.
- In the Quick Actions panel, a new feature allows you to use Adobe AI to instantly improve compressed JPEG files.
- Clicking the Fine Tune button after applying a Quick Action allows you to adjust the outcome.

Creating Stylized Text (Add Text Guided Edit)

ADD TEXT guided edit: Create visually appealing text for posts that are worth sharing. Text can be aligned vertically, horizontally, or on a route or shape. Use patterns and gradients to warp and style it.

To use this guided edit, take the following actions:

1. Choose from the following options:

- Launch Photoshop Elements and open a photo.
- Choose a picture from the photo Bin.

2. Go to Basics > Guided mode > ADD TEXT.

3. Choose one of the following types of tools from the right panel:

- Text entry is possible horizontally with the help of the horizontal type tool.
- It is possible to enter text vertically with the Vertical Type Tool.
- Text on Selection Tool: Enables you to enter text around the quick selection's boundaries by doing a rapid selection.
- T+
- +
- **Text on Shape Tool:** This tool lets you add text to the edges of a custom shape that's drawn over an image.
- Text on Path Tool: This tool lets you type text to go around the edge of a personalized path that is drawn over the picture.

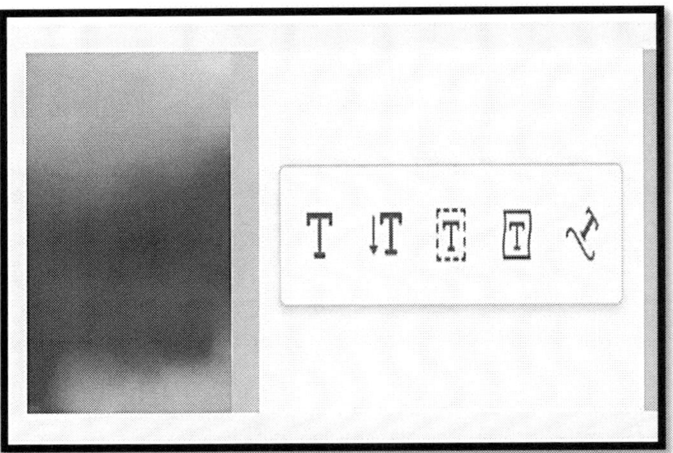

Note: The Tool settings panel contains several formatting settings that you may experiment with, including fonts, font styles, sizes, colors, leading, tracking, and text alignment.

4. Text can be further customized by choosing the appropriate Style, Bend, Horizontal Distortion, and Vertical Distortion from the Warp Text dialog box after choosing the Create Warped Text icon from the action bar.

5. Add a text style with stroke, bevel, and shadow to it.

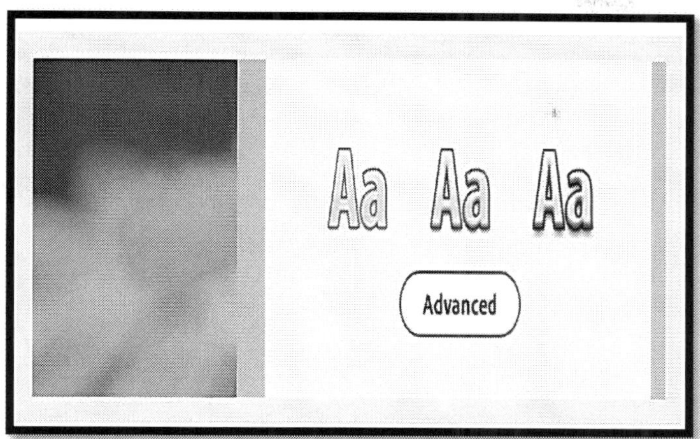

Note: By choosing the advanced button in the Style Settings panel, you can further alter the text style according to your unique needs.

6. Text can be made more visually appealing by adding a gradient or pattern.

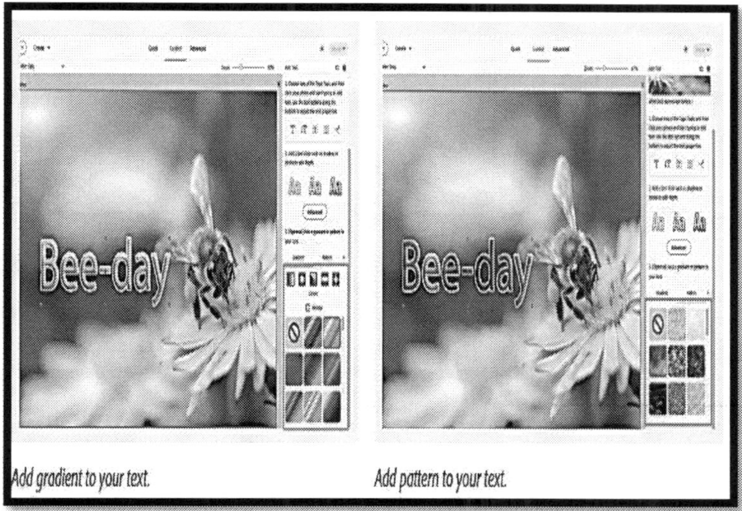

Add gradient to your text. Add pattern to your text.

7. Choose Next to decide how you want to continue after you've achieved the desired outcome:

- Preserve the newly made photo with stylized text in any format that is accessible by selecting Save - Save/Save As.

- In Quick/Advanced mode, carry on editing: Decide whether to work in Quick mode or Advanced mode to continue editing the photo with stylized text.
- Share - Flickr: Using Photoshop Elements, you may choose which social media or sharing platform to use to post your image with stylized text.

Advanced Typing Tools

Employ the Text on Selection option.

Enables you to enter text around the fast selection's boundaries by performing a rapid selection.

The Text on Selection tool can be used by following these steps:

1. To use the Text on Selection type tool, choose it.
2. Choose the region of the image where you want to put the text by dragging the pointer over it.
Note: To adjust the selection tool's size, enclose the value in square brackets.
3. Click the Commit current operation button to verify your selection.
4. Drag the mouse pointer over the selected area's border until the Type tool icon appears instead of the Text on Selection type tool icon, then click over the boundary to display the reference text over the selected area. Type the desired text to begin adding it. To further suit your needs, you can alter the reference text further.
5. Click on the Commit current operation button to store the content, and select the Cancel current operation button to reverse the modifications.

Apply the Text on the Shape Tool

Enables the custom shape to be drawn over the image and allows you to insert the desired text around its edge.

Use the Text on Shape tool by following these steps:

1. Choose the Text on Shape type tool.

2. Choose the preferred custom shape from the Tool Options to apply the text. To make the shape, drag the cursor over the image.

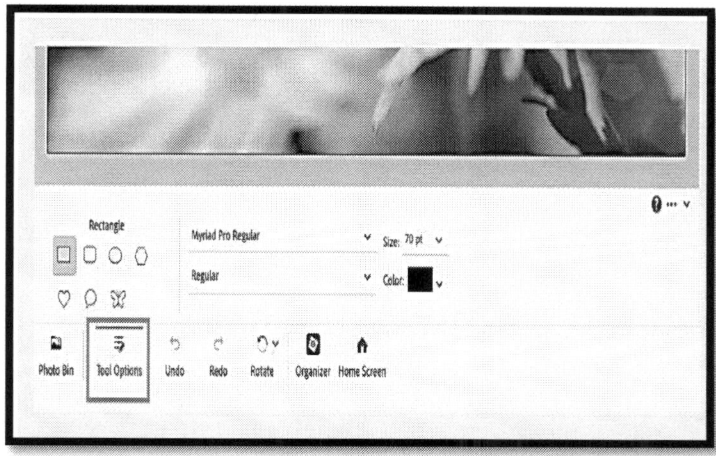

3. Move the mouse pointer over the selected shape's boundary until the Text on Shape type tool icon changes to the Type tool icon. Then, click over the chosen shape's boundary to display the reference text over the chosen shape. Type the desired text to begin adding it. To further suit your needs, you can alter the reference text further.

4. Click on the Commit current operation button to store the content, and select the Cancel current operation button to reverse the modifications.

Utilize the Text on Path tool.

Allows the custom path to be drawn over the image and allows you to insert the desired text around its perimeter.

Use the Text on Path tool by following these steps:

1. Choose the Text on Path type tool.

2. Sketch the outline of the picture that you want the text to appear over.

3. To verify the path, use the button labeled Commit current operation.

4. To obtain the reference text over the selected region, move the mouse pointer over the drawn path until the Text on Path type tool icon changes to the Type tool icon. Then, click over the path's border. To add the desired text, start typing. The reference text can be further altered based on your needs.

5. To save the text, select the Commit current operation button; to reverse the changes, select the Cancel current operation button.

Object Removal guided edit

You can eliminate extraneous elements from your images with the **OBJECT REMOVAL** guided edit.

This is how it's done:

1. Choose one of the following actions:

- Launch Photoshop Elements and open a picture.
- From the Photo Bin, choose a picture.

2. Choose Object Removal under Basics > Guided mode.

3. Choose one of these selection tools from the right panel:

- Paint: Apply paint to the object you wish to erase using the Selection Brush tool. The brush's size can be changed by utilizing the Brush Size slider.
- Lasso-Make a free-form selection around the item you wish to remove by using the Lasso tool.

- Auto- Make a selection when you draw a shape around an object to be removed by using the Auto Selection tool.
- Quick: When you select drag the object you wish to remove, use the Quick Selection tool to make a selection based on edges. The Brush Size slider can be used to change the Quick Selection tool's dimensions.

Matching Color and Tone For a Fresh new vibe

Photoshop Elements 2024 has a new option called matching color and tone that enables you to give your photographs a whole new look. After selecting one of the pre-made presets or using your photo, you can adjust hue, saturation, and brightness. You can experiment with various styles and moods or create a consistent appearance and feel for your images with the help of this tool.

Use the following procedures to make use of this feature:

- Open a picture and choose the Expert mode.
- Drag the Background layer to the New Layer icon in the Layers panel to duplicate it.
- Choose Enhance > Match Color and Tone after selecting the duplicate layer.
- In the Match Color and Tone dialog box, you can choose a preset from the drop-down menu, or click on the Browse button to select a photo from your computer or Adobe Stock.
- Adjust the Hue, Saturation, and Brightness sliders to fine-tune the effect.
- Click OK to apply the changes.

Select a Sky or Background with one Click

Select the Background, Sky, or Subject in your picture automatically with a single click. To detect the Subject, Sky, or Background in your shot, Photoshop Elements leverages Adobe Sensei AI technology.

The one-click selection choices can be accessed by following these steps:

1. Choose File > Open or Open in the Quick or Advanced workspace to view the desired image.

2. Choose from the following two workflows to get the one-click selection options:

- Select Sky, Background, or Subject from the choices under the Select menu.

- Select any tool from the Tools panel to begin the selection process. Then, use the action bar to select an option from Subject, Sky, or Background.

3. Give Photoshop Elements a few seconds to choose the Background, Subject, or Sky on your image automatically. Marching ants, or a moving, dotted line, will make the selection visible.

Access Free Adobe stock photos

Adobe Stock images are now available in both Quick and Advanced modes from the File menu. To incorporate Adobe Stock photos into your projects, adhere to the following steps:

1. Choose File > Search in either Quick or Advanced mode on Adobe Stock.

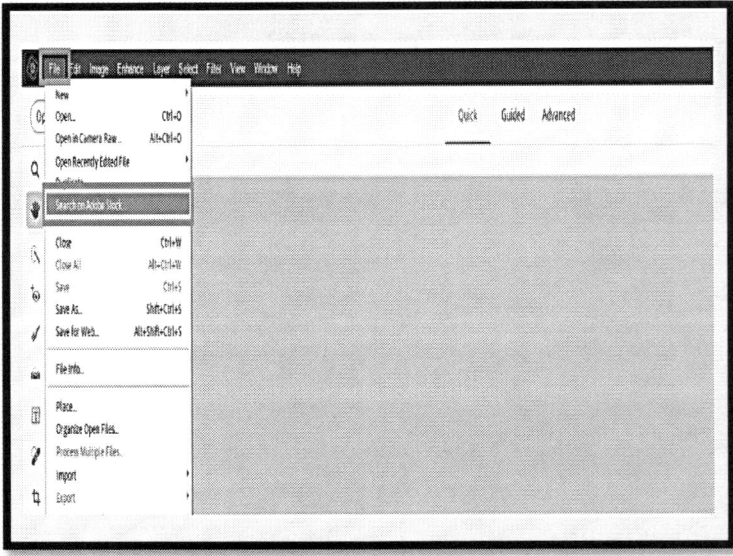

2. Search through multiple categories in the Adobe Stock dialog box to locate the desired image. Additionally, you can use the search bar to look for particular photos by entering keywords.

Note: To view a preview of the selected photo, select the thumbnail.

3. Click the License for Free option to download the image and obtain a free license.

In the Advanced Setting

Utilize Adobe Stock Photo in your projects by following these steps:

1. Select File > Open. Go to the Advanced mode to view the selected image.

2. Toggle between Adobe Stock and Graphics panel.

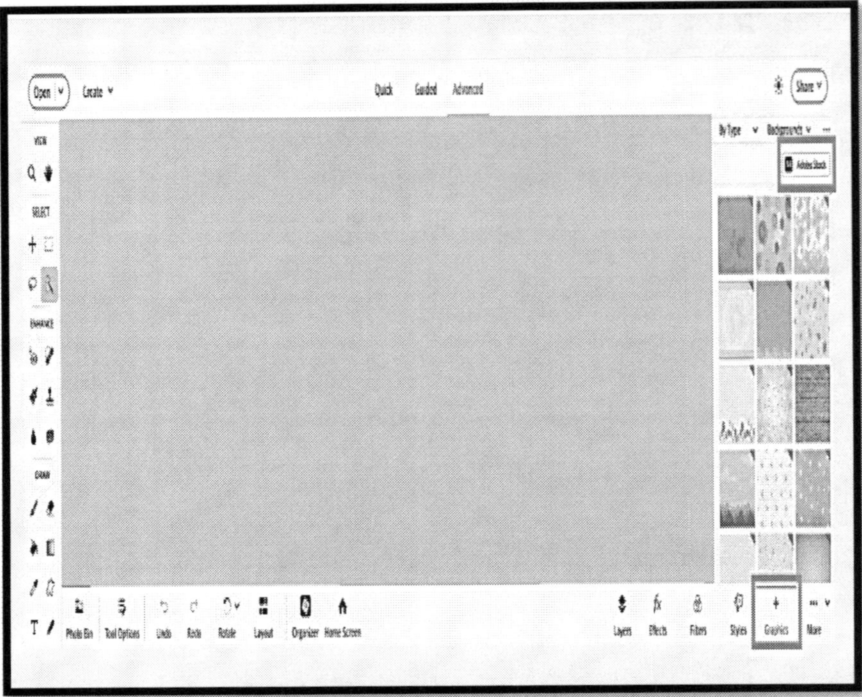

3. In the Adobe Stock dialog box, browse through several categories to locate the desired image. The search bar can also be used to look for particular photos by entering keywords.

Note: To view the chosen photo, select the thumbnail.

4. The photo can be downloaded and licensed for free by selecting the License for free option.

5. Choose Layers to see the background layer application of the Adobe Stock photo.

Quote Graphic

Utilize Adobe Stock Photo in your projects by following these steps:

1. Navigate to Create > Quote Graphic.

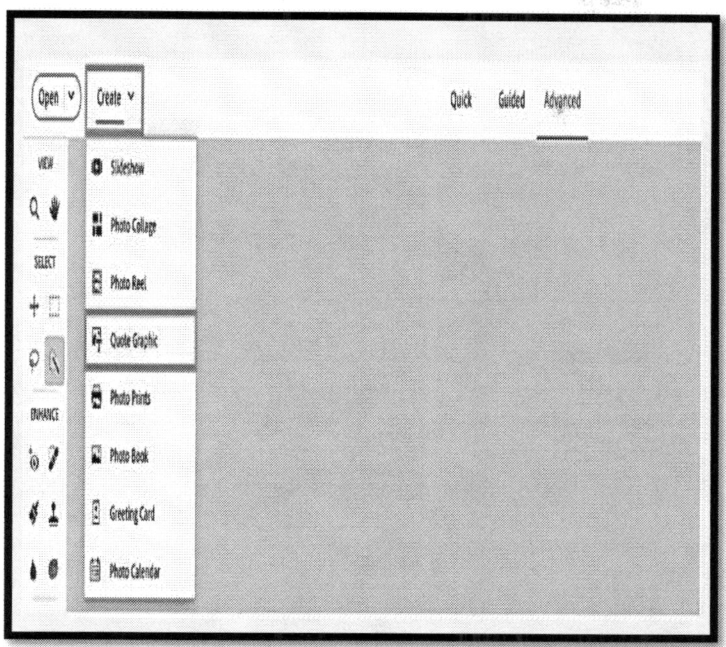

2. You have the option to select from the custom templates or upload your photo by clicking on the Start with a photo option.

3. The Backgrounds panel will appear; select Adobe Stock.

4. In the Adobe Stock dialog box, browse through several categories to locate the desired image. The search bar can also be used to look for particular photos by entering keywords.

5. The photo can be downloaded and licensed for free by selecting the License for free option.

6. The selected image will become the Adobe Stock background instead of your default background.

Add Creative overlays in the web companion App

The images you've saved in the cloud may now be used to create Pattern Overlay artwork.

1. Select the Pattern Overlay card after going to the Creations screen.

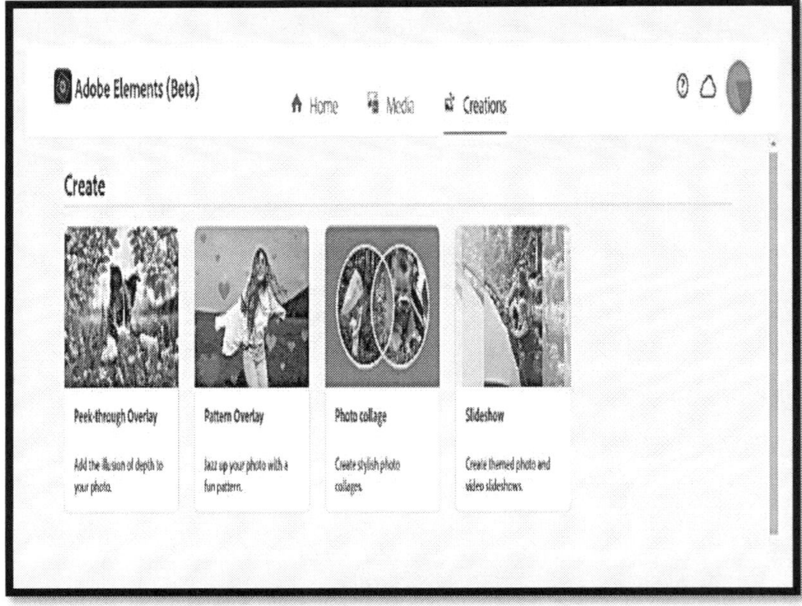

2. Also, by selecting the preferred media and clicking the Create button in the action bar, you may make Pattern Overlay creations straight from the Media screen.

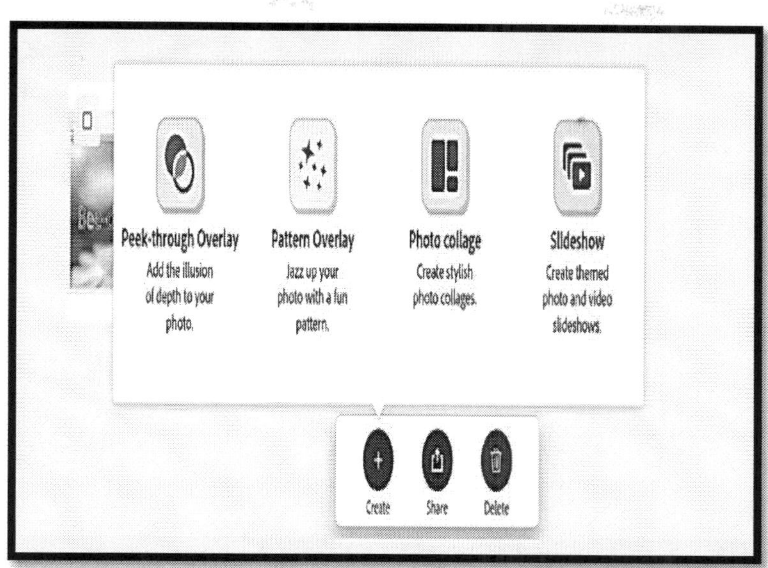

3. A variety of Pattern Overlay Presets made using your picture will be shown as soon as you join the process. Tap them to get a preview in full screen.

4. Replace Media may be used from inside the creation to swap out the image and suggest another picture for a pattern overlay.

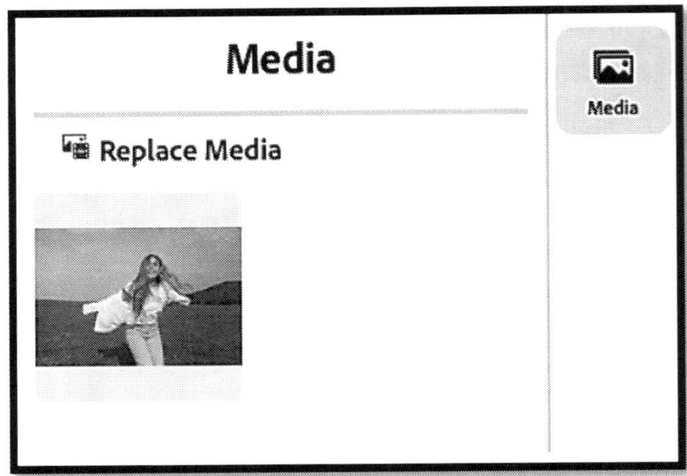

5. When finished, you may save your works as JPG or PNG files and send them over to Facebook by email or URL. Furthermore, if you want to store the project and come back to it later, you may use the store option.

Create Peek-through Overlay creations

Now, you can employ the images you've saved in the cloud to create peek-through overlay creations. With Peek-through Overlay, you can add realistic overlays of flowers, leaves, grass, and other natural elements to your subject to give the appearance of depth in any photograph.

1. Select the Peek-through Overlay card after going to the Creations screen.
2. By selecting the suitable media > Select make button from the action bar, you may easily make Peek-through Overlay creations straight from the Media panel.
3. As soon as you get into the process, you may choose and edit several Peek-through Overlay settings for your image.

4. To change the image and create Peek-through Overlay suggestions for a different image, choose change Media from inside the project.

5. Using the Layout tab, you can customize your output to make it simple to share on social media or print.

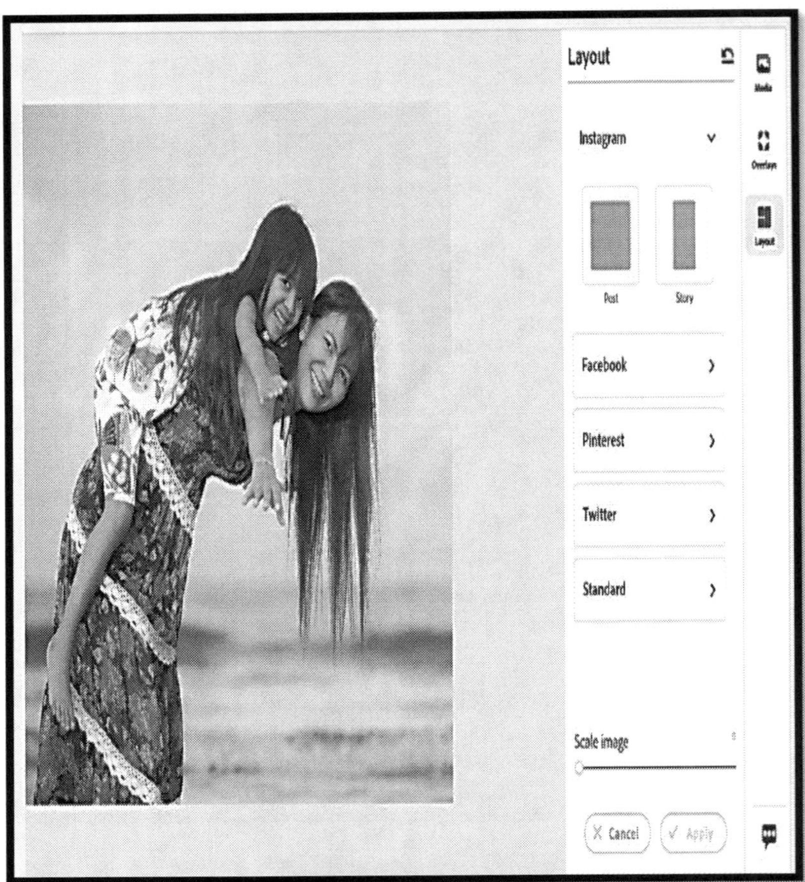

6. After finishing, you may send your works to Facebook by email or a link, or you can save them as JPG or PNG files. To save the project and change it later, you may also use the Save option.

CHAPTER THREE

UNLOCKING THE WORLD OF IMAGE EDITING

Acquaint Yourself with Photoshop Elements Home Screen

Photoshop Element's Home Screen contains collages and slideshows made from imported photos and movies. It's also a great way to discover new writing projects, get ideas, visit other places, look at recently posted work, and get help.

The search box located at the top of the home screen can be used by users to find useful tutorials and support resources. When you type in certain terms and press Enter, the search tool shows images and links to results that match on the Home screen. When a user clicks on an image or link, a computer browser accesses the webpage. To go back to the Home Screen, just click the Home link, which is situated in the top left corner of the screen.

The card carousel in the upper portion of the Home Screen provides you with access to the newest ideas, projects, and features. Use the left and right arrows to navigate this slideshow. The most recent features of Photoshop Element are shown on cards that have a blue tag that says "what's new." To see them, users may click the open Links button by moving the mouse cursor over the What's New card.

Cards with the words "Inspiration" or "Explore" on them (shown by an orange tag) link visitors to sites that provide examples of how other users have used certain features. By clicking the View button and moving the mouse cursor over the orange cards, users may access these tools. Alternatively, you may try out useful features using the "Try This" cards (designated with green tags). Photoshop Elements opens and guides you through each step when you point and click on a feature card.

When you input media to Photoshop Element, it generates Auto Creations, such as image collages, slideshows, video collages, and candid moments. Users may see these works by clicking the open button next to any auto creation that is shown. To examine all of the potential creations, click to Examine All button below the Auto-generated picture, or use the number of icons below the image to choose a particular creation. Additionally, you may use Photoshop Element's home screen to reach other sites. Clicking the organizer button causes the organizer window to open. This makes it easier to add, browse, and arrange photographs in your image library, ensuring optimal functionality and organization. In a similar vein, selecting the Photo Editor Button opens the Photo Editor window, which has a wide range of editing and image creation possibilities. Clicking the Video Editor button in Adobe Photoshop Element Premiere brings up the video editing area.

The Recent Files feature on the Home Screen also makes it easy to see previously used project files. It can hold up to six project files. By clicking on the links to these files, users may access them instantaneously. Users may click the close button in Photoshop Element's upper right corner to dismiss the window and leave the Home screen. They may go back to the Home screen by hitting the Home screen button on the Taskbar of the Photo Editor or Organizer window. You may also close and reopen the Element app to go back to the Home Screen.

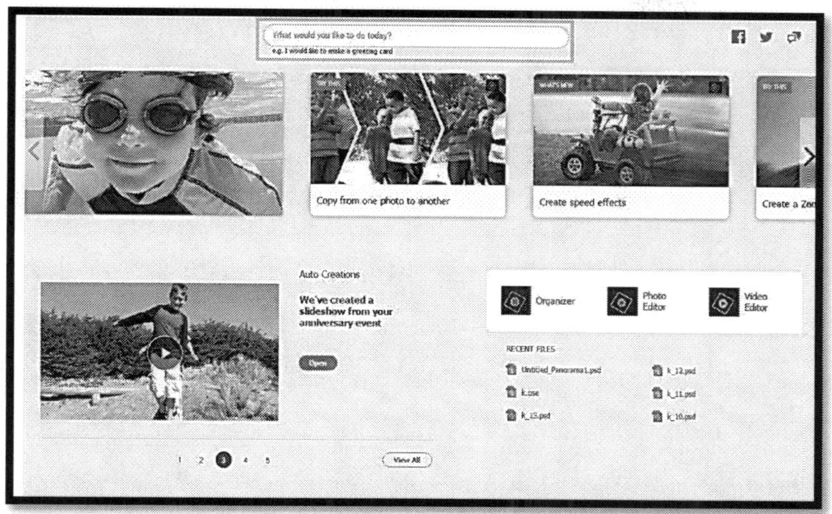

Open your desired Elements application

The Home screen is where you may launch any of the three Elements applications. To access and use the chosen Elements app, click its icon. The following may be accessed from the Home screen:

To develop and work with picture projects, use Adobe Photoshop Elements (picture Editor) and Elements Organizer (Organizer) to import and manage media (photos and videos).

Utilizing Adobe Premiere Elements (Video Editor) to produce and manage video content

Components of Photoshop Elements

Explore the diverse components that make Photoshop Elements 2024 an indispensable tool for photographers and enthusiasts alike.

Organizer Module: Effortlessly manage your photo and video library with the Organizer module. Import, categorize, and arrange your media for quick and easy access. Create custom albums, apply tags, and assign ratings to streamline your file organization process. The Organizer module serves as the hub where you can effortlessly keep track of your growing collection.

Photo Editor Hub: Dive into the heart of image editing with the Photo Editor module, where a range of modes – Quick, Guided, and Expert – cater to users of all skill levels. Unleash your creativity using an extensive toolkit that includes various tools, filters, effects, and layer options. Whether you're a novice or an expert, the Photo Editor provides a seamless editing experience, allowing you to transform your photos with precision and finesse.

Create Module: Transform your photos into captivating projects with the Create module. Craft stunning slideshows, vibrant collages, personalized calendars, and heartwarming greeting cards. This module offers a plethora of options to breathe life into your images, allowing you to print or share your creations online effortlessly. Elevate your projects with a touch of personalization and creativity.

Auto Creations Showcase: Witness the magic of automated creativity with the Auto Creations feature. Photoshop Elements 2024 generates stunning photo collages, dynamic slideshows, and engaging memes with ease. Dive into the Auto Creations showcase to view and customize these automatic masterpieces, adding a touch of personal flair to the results.

Starting Simple Edits on Quick Mode

Quick Edit Mode in Photoshop Elements is a function that enables you to make simple alterations to your photographs with only a few clicks. You may crop, rotate, resize, enhance, and rectify your photographs using the tools and settings in the Panel Bin. To switch to Quick Edit Mode, click "Quick" in the Shortcuts Bar. To apply a fast fix modification, click the drop-down next to the repair's name and use the buttons, sliders, and other controls to make your adjustments. You can also compare your altered picture with the original by clicking the View option.

The Quick mode allows you to rapidly adjust an image's exposure, color, sharpness, and other elements by combining common photo-fixing tools in one location. The Effects, Quick Actions, Textures, and Frames panels—which are located adjacent to the Adjustments panel—allow you to further alter your images.

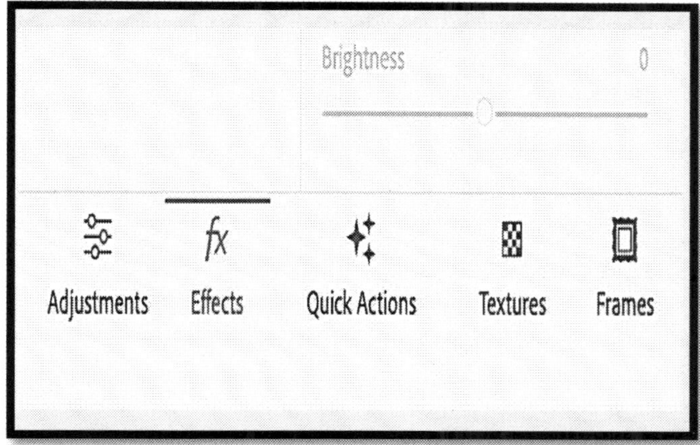

Effects

The Effects panel offers a single place from which you may apply picture effects. The Effects panel is available on the taskbar in Quick and Advanced mode. It offers thumbnail samples of the artwork or effects that you may add or apply to a picture. Most sections give a menu of category selections and accompanying subcategories. There are three sorts of effects, you may pick from: Artistic, Classic, and Color Match.

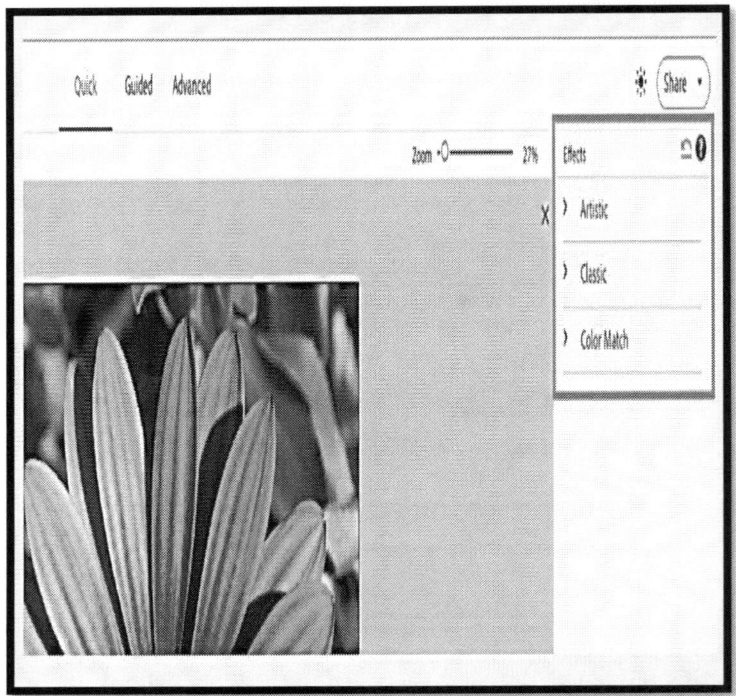

Artistic Effects

Transform your photographs with effects modeled by well-known paintings or prominent art movements with just a single click. Select from a variety of breathtaking artistic effects to add to all or a portion of your image, then simply edit the outcome to get the precise appearance you like. Both Quick and Advanced modes give you access to these creative effects.

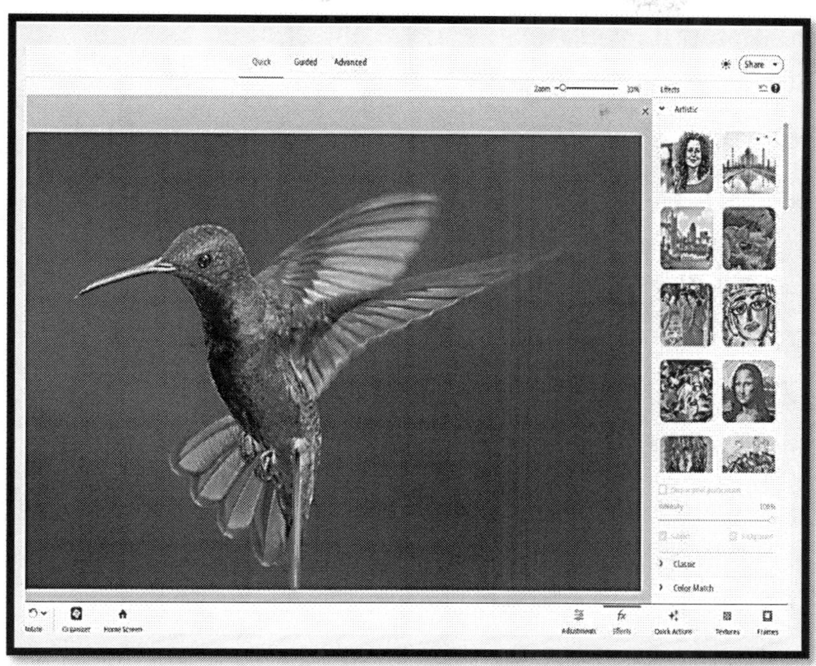

Classic effects

There are 55 classic effects, including cross-process presets, vintage styles, and black-and-white options. To see the possible variants inside the preset, choose one of the Classic effects.

After applying the time-tested Smart Look effect in Quick mode, enhance your photographs with Classic effects.

A summary of every effect that is accessible is given in the list below:

Automatic Smart Looks

Examine the given picture, analyze it, and offer alternatives with various effects applied depending on the image content. Available alternatives:

Auto1, Auto2, Auto3, Auto4, and Auto5

Note: Using a layer mask, effects are applied as a new layer. To lessen or eliminate effects from certain regions, you may alter the layer mask in advanced mode.

Tint

Gives the picture a certain color tint (such as green, sepia, or golden).
Obtainable variants
Gold. Copper, Sepia, Green, Blue

Seasons

Adds a seasonal touch to the picture. Available variations:
Spring, Summer, Fall, Winter, and Snow

Pencil Sketch

Adds a technique to give the picture the appearance of a pencil drawing. Available variations:

Soft Pencil Sketch: Charcoal Stippling, Colored Pencil

Toy Camera

Applies a technique that gives the impression that the picture was captured with a toy camera. Available variations:
Blue Toy Camera Lomo, Lomo Green Holga Lomo Contrast

Black & White

Applies a black-and-white effect to the picture. Variations that are accessible:
Simple B & W Silver, Vintage Platinum Tinted Black

Lithograph

Gives the picture the appearance of a lithograph. Available alternatives: Black Sepia, Copper, Blue, Green

Cross Process

Demonstrates the impact of processing photographic film in a chemical solution meant for a different kind of film. Available variations: Orange with Deep Blue Wash, Purple Wash, Green Wash, and Blue Wash.

Split Tone

Applies the effect of applying a different color to the shadows and a different color to the highlights in a black-and-white picture. Available variations:

Split Tone, Bluish tone, Red, Green, and Grey tones

Vintage

Provides the picture with a vintage look. Obtainable variants

Vintage Leak

Faded Vintage

Vintage Color

Sepia Glow

Heavy Vintage

Light Leaks

Describes how light enters a camera's light-tight chamber and affects the negative of an image that has leaked. Available alternatives: Burnt edges, diffused colors, Gentle Seepage, White Seepage, Yellow Streak.

Color Match effects

Select from pre-made presets or upload your image. Further adjustments may be made to brightness, saturation, and color. Examine the Quick and Advanced versions of the Color Match effect.

Use the Color Match effect in the quick mode.

1. To open a picture over which you want to apply the effect, choose File > Open or click the Open button.

2. Select settings that are already included in the Color Match inside the Effects panel.

Note: Since layers are not introduced, Color Match effects are mutually exclusive. Any presets applied to the primary input picture will be replaced by the effect of another preset.

One of the following two methods can be used to apply one preset over another: When using the next preset, save the result of the previous one and use it as the input picture. Apply the first preset in Quick mode, then go to Advanced mode. In Advanced mode, use the Quick mode result as your input picture, then choose the preset you want to apply.

3. Depending on what you need, you may adjust your photo's brightness, hue, and saturation further.

Note: To reverse the modifications, choose the Undo button. To reverse the edits, select the Redo button.

4. To save the picture, choose File > Save As. To post it on social media, choose Share.

Textures

Select one of ten available textures for your picture using the Textures window. Textures simulate different backdrops or surfaces that the image could have been printed on. Consider textures such as cracked paint, rough blue grid, and aged paper appearance and feel.

Frames

Choose and apply any available frames for your picture using the Frames panel. The optimal fitting of the frame is automatically performed. Both the picture and the frame may be moved or altered. To do this, double-click the frame while holding down the move tool. With the Color Fill layer modified in advanced mode, you may swap out the white backdrop with any other color you admire.

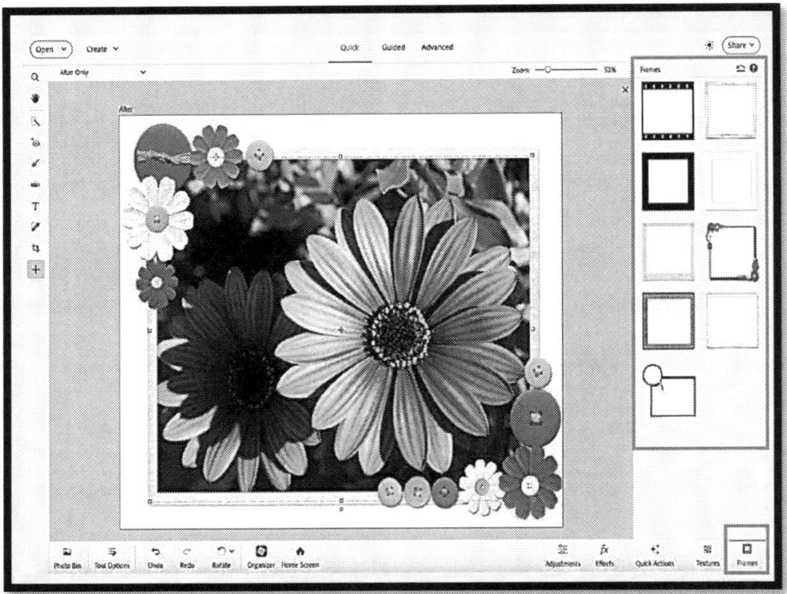

Retracing Image Editing Steps

There may be situations when you make a mistake throughout the process of editing your photographs or you may just not like the change you have made. You may rapidly retrace your operations by using the Undo and Redo commands.

• Click the edit menu and undo (Ctrl + Z) or Redo (Ctrl +Y) to retrace your move backward or forward.

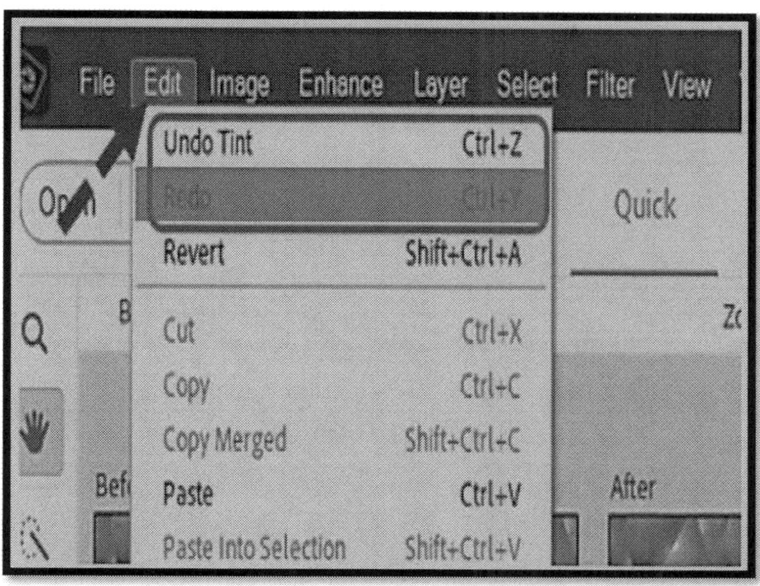

Retracing Editing via the History panel

While working on a specific photo or project, the history panel aids in detailing the editing history. With a thorough description of the modifications that have been made to the picture or image, you can scroll up and down in the history panel to produce adjustments during the present work session.

Follow these procedures to access the history Panel:

- Click the Window menu and pick History to open the history panel.

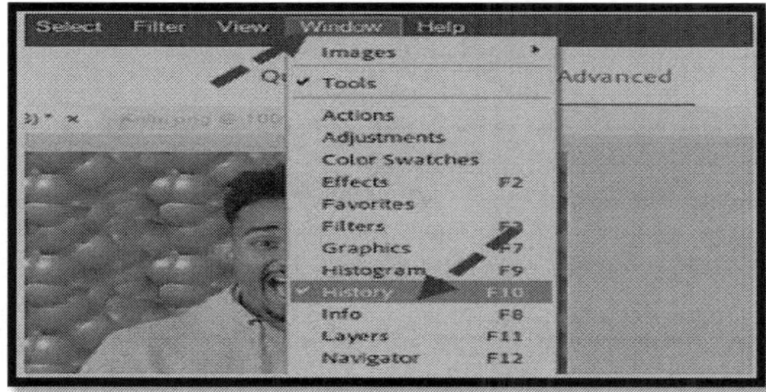

- The list of the alterations that have been made to the present picture is enumerated below.

Reverting to the previous State of an Image

Three simple methods may be used to return a photograph to its prior condition, either in the Quick or Advanced modes. These methods are outlined below.

- Method A: Utilize the Edit Menu's Undo and Redo

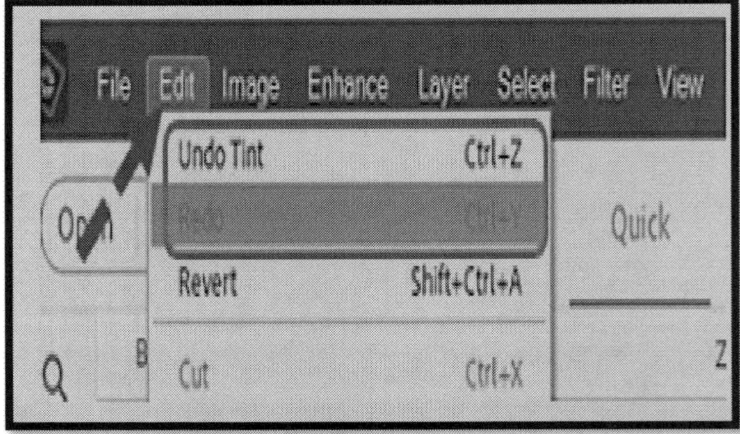

- Method B: Make use of the Taskbar's Undo and Redo buttons.

- Method C: In the History Panel, click the state.

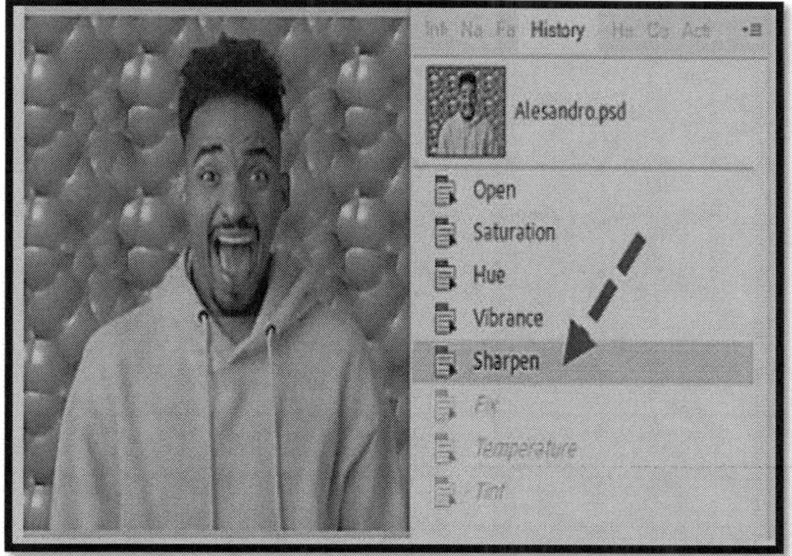

Reverting to the Last Save

All changes and adjustments are lost when you go back to the previous save, leaving the image in its original state.

To undo using the Revert command, do the following actions:

- Select Revert from the Edit menu.

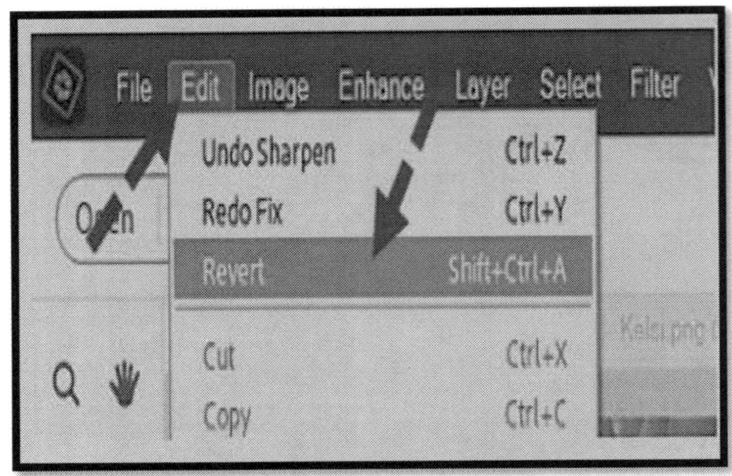

Erasing and deleting states from the History panel

To remove any adjustment from the list that you no longer need for your image, use the following actions:

• Hover your cursor over the action, and choose Delete from the History panel menu.

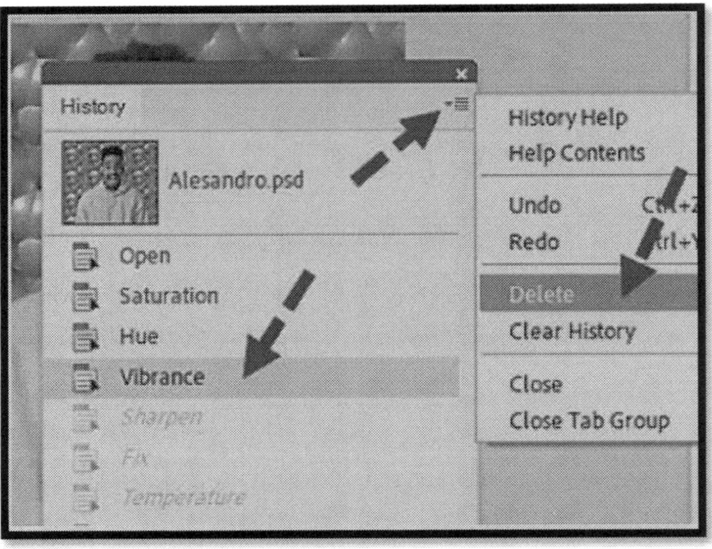

- Next, choose "yes" when the offer to authorize the deletion appears.

If you want to remove the states list from the history panel without altering the appearance, follow the methods listed below.

• Drag your mouse over the activity, and choose "Clear History" from the options in the history panel.

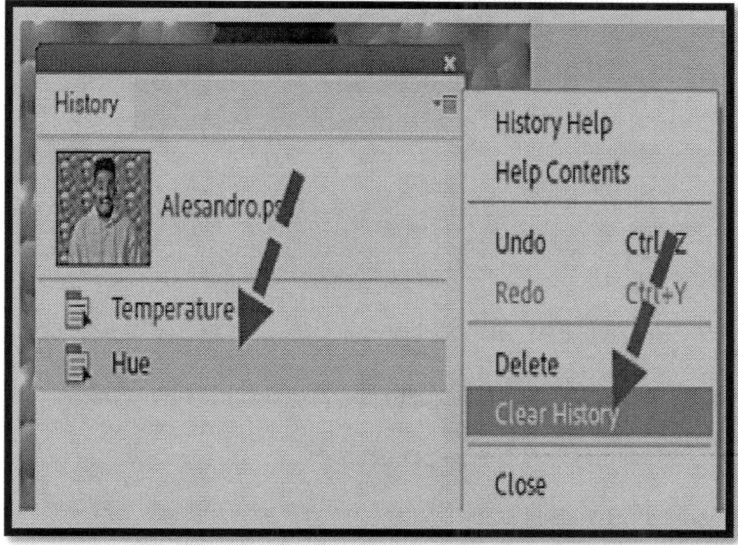

Exploring Elements Help Commands

While using Photoshop Element, you can run into issues and want assistance. Here are several Adobe-supplied resources that you may use in this situation.

The Menu for Help

The first place to go for guidance in Photoshop is the help menu, which makes it easier to access all of the information available. In the Photo Editor or Organizer interface, the help menu may be found on the far right side of the menu bar. You can get the help you need by using the instructions that appear when you click the help menu.

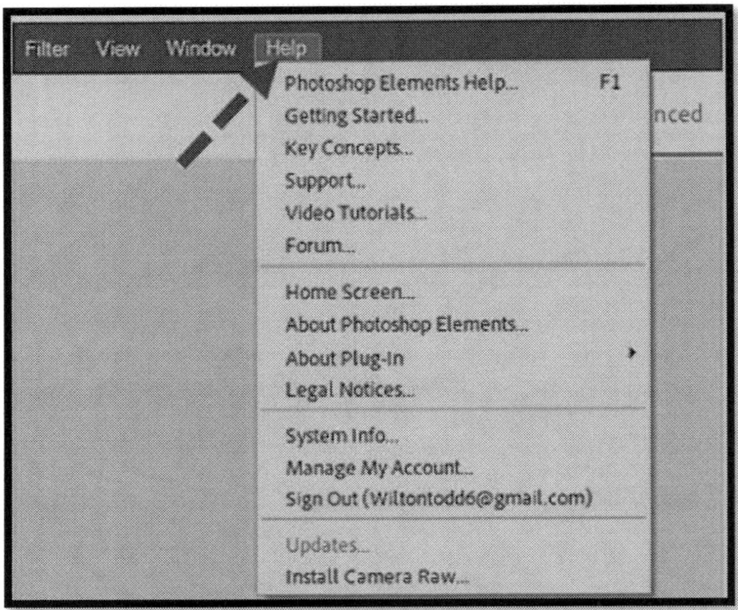

We will now examine a few of the help menu commands.

Photoshop Element Help: This opens a window for you to type in the keyword of what you're looking for. To access the Element Help file, use the shortcut key F1.

Starting Point: By selecting this option, you may acquire tips and information on how to get started using Photoshop Elements. This order has great strength and helps you stay on course.

Key Concepts: This command might be useful if you come across a term or phrase that you don't understand. When you click this command, your default web browser will open and a website explaining the principles will appear, along with links to other online resources.

Support: By selecting the support command, you may go to the Adobe website. On the Adobe website, you may get the most recent information regarding Elements, user-reported issues, and helpful tips for making the most of Adobe Elements. The Adobe website has information that may help improve the use of Adobe Element and provide a variety of solutions for any problems that may arise.

Video Tutorials: To access a page on Adobe's website with many videos that will help you use the Adobe Element, click the video tutorials command.

Forum: Select this command to launch a page with user questions, comments, and solutions to common problems that crop up while using Photoshop Element.

Using Mouse Tips

Additional assistance options will appear as text underneath your cursor whenever you move your mouse over any object in the Photoshop Element. The text being pointed at is described in the displayed texts.

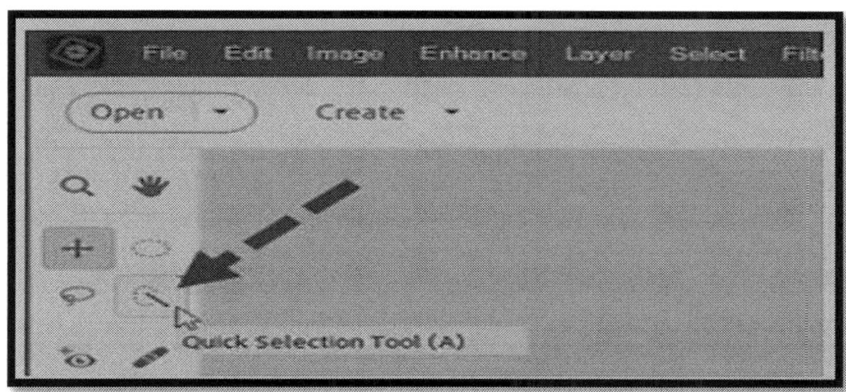

Saving Files for Various Reasons

Using Save/ Save As

The File menu's Save as option allows you to specify parameters for saving picture files, such as the format, whether to add the saved file to the Elements Organizer catalog, and whether to keep layers in the image intact. You may be able to configure additional settings based on the format you choose.

Choose from the following options:

- Choose File > Save As.
- Optionally, use Command+Shift+S (Mac OS) or Ctrl+Shift+S (Windows).
- Click Save after adjusting the following file-saving parameters:

Note: Certain file types pop up an additional dialog box with further settings.

Add the Elements Organizer

Adds the saved file to your collection so the picture appears in the Picture Browser. In the Elements Organizer, several file types that are supported in the Edit workspace are not supported. This option isn't accessible if you save a file in one of these formats, such as EPS.

Save With Original Version Set

Saves the file and then adds it to a version set in the Photo Browser so that the many picture versions are kept in order. If Include in the Organizer is not chosen, this option is not accessible.

Layers: Holds onto every layer of the picture. The picture has no layers if this option is deactivated or not accessible. When you pick a format, the layers in your picture will either be merged or flattened, as indicated by a warning symbol at the Layers check box. All of the layers are combined in certain forms. Choose an alternative format to maintain the layers.

As a copy

Keeps the active file open while saving a duplicate of it. The copy is stored in the folder where the open file is located at the moment.

The ICC Profile

Add a color profile to the picture for certain file types.

Saves the file's thumbnail information. When the Ask when saving option for Image Previews is enabled in the Preferences dialog box, this option becomes accessible.

Employ Lower Case Extension

Changes the file extension from lowercase to uppercase.

SAVING USING DIFFERENT FILE FORMATS

Portable Network Graphics (PNG)

1. Navigate to File > Save As.
2. Use the keyboard shortcut Ctrl+Shift+S (Windows) or Command+Shift+S (Mac OS).
3. From the format list, choose PNG.

Specify a desired file name and location, customize file-saving options, and then click Save.

Within the PNG Options dialog box, opt for an Interlace setting and click OK.

- None: This option exhibits the image solely in a web browser after its complete download.
- Interlaced: This choice presents low-resolution versions of the image while the full file is being downloaded to the browser. Interlacing can create the perception of a shorter download time and inform viewers that the download is in progress. However, it's important to note that interlacing also leads to an increase in file size.

Joint Photographers Experts Group (JPEG)

- Choose File > Save As.
- On Windows, press Ctrl+Shift+S; on Mac OS, press Command+Shift+S.

Select JPEG from the list of available formats.

Note: Bitmap and indexed-color images cannot be saved in JPEG format. After choosing a file name, location, and file-saving option, click Save.

A dialog window with JPEG options will appear.

- Choose a Matte hue to replicate the effect of background transparency if the image contains any transparency.
- Select an option from the Quality menu, adjust the Quality slider, or input a number between 1 and 12 to determine the picture's compression and quality.

JPEG Format Options:

- Baseline ("Standard"): This format is widely recognized by most web browsers.

- Optimized Baseline: Reduces file size slightly while optimizing color quality. Note that this option is not supported by all web browsers.
- Progressive: Generates an image that loads progressively in a web browser. Progressive JPEG files may not be compatible with all applications and web browsers, have a slightly larger file size, and require more RAM for display.

Once your selections are made, press OK.

Tag Image File Format (TIFF)

1. Select File > Save As.
2. On Windows, use Ctrl+Shift+S; on Mac OS, press Command+Shift+S.

Choose TIFF from the list of available formats.

Click Save after specifying a file name, location, and file-saving option.

In the TIFF Settings dialog box, configure the following settings:

- **Compression of Images**: Defines the compression strategy for the composite picture data.
- **Order of Pixels:** To add the picture to the Elements Organizer, choose Interleaved.
- **Order of Bytes:** Most modern programs can read files in either Windows or Mac byte order. If unsure about the application that will open the file, choose the platform on which the file will be read.
- **Save Image Pyramid:** Retains data in multiple resolutions. While Photoshop Elements opens the picture at the maximum resolution included in the file, Adobe InDesign® and some image servers support opening multiresolution files.

- **Preserve Openness:** Maintains transparency as an additional alpha channel when the file is opened in a different program. Transparency is always retained in Photoshop Elements upon reopening the file.
- **Layer Compression:** Describes a method to compress layer data (as opposed to composite data) for pixels. Many programs may ignore layer data when reading a TIFF file, but Photoshop Elements can interpret TIFF file layer data. Saving layer data eliminates the need to create and maintain a separate PSD file to preserve layer data, even if files with layer data are larger than those without.

Once configured, press OK to apply the settings.

Photoshop (PDF) Portable Document Format

1. Choose File > Save As.
2. On Windows, press Ctrl+Shift+S; on Mac OS, press Command+Shift+S.

Select Photoshop PDF from the available formats.

Click Save after specifying a file name, location, and file-saving option.

In the Save Adobe PDF dialog box, choose a compression technique (refer to Understanding compressed files).

- Select a setting from the menu to determine image quality.

Depending on whether the program is installed on your computer, choose to view the PDF after saving by selecting "See PDF After Saving." This action will open Adobe Acrobat or Adobe® Reader to display the PDF file.

Finally, select "Save PDF" to complete the process.

Photoshop (PSD)

1. Navigate to the menu and select File > Save As.
2. From the format list, opt for Photoshop (PSD) to retain all layers and editing information.
3. Click Save to preserve your file in PSD format.

Saving Files for the Web

1. Choose File > Export > Save for Web (Legacy) to optimize the file for online display.
2. Select a suitable file format, such as JPEG or PNG, depending on your preferences.
3. Adjust quality settings to balance file size and image quality.
4. Specify the desired image size for online presentation.
5. Click Save to save the file, optimized for web display.

CHAPTER FOUR

GETTING PREPARED FOR IMAGE EDITING

Picture Elements (Pixels)

Pixels serve as the fundamental building blocks of digital images, forming the visual composition on your screen with these small color squares. The clarity and detail of your picture depend on the quantity of pixels it contains, referred to as its resolution.

In Photoshop Elements 2024, various methods allow you to manipulate pixels. For instance, you can:

1. **Resize:** Adjust the pixel count or overall dimensions of your picture using the Image Size dialog box.
2. **Crop:** Remove unnecessary pixels from the edges of your picture using either the Crop Tool or the Crop Guided Edit.
3. **Edit Single or Multiple Pixels:** Modify individual or groups of pixels with tools such as the Brush, Clone Stamp, Eraser, Healing Brush, and others.
4. **Select Pixels:** Utilize tools like the Magic Wand, Lasso, Quick Selection, and Selection Brush to choose pixels based on their color, shape, or position.
5. **Transform Pixels:** Apply various transformations, including scaling, skewing, warping, or rotating, using the Transform Guided Edit or the Free Transform command.
6. **Apply Effects:** Filter individual pixels with effects such as blur, sharpening, noise, creativity, or sketch using the Filter Gallery or the Filter Guided Edit.

Image Resolution

The image size, often referred to as pixel dimensions, defines the number of pixels along the width and height of an image. For instance, a digital camera might capture an image that is 1500 pixels wide and 1000 pixels high, indicating the quantity of picture data and influencing the resulting file size.

The resolution, measured in pixels per inch (PPI), signifies the amount of picture data within a specific space. A higher pixel-per-inch count correlates with better resolution, and generally, a higher resolution enhances the printed image quality. The resolution also impacts the level of detail and sharpness perceivable in an image.

While a digital image possesses a precise quantity of visual data, it lacks a predetermined physical output size or resolution. Adjusting the resolution alters the image's physical dimensions, and modifying the width or height also changes its resolution.

Considerations about picture size and resolution become apparent when using the Picture Size dialog box (accessible through Image > Resize > Image Size). Modifying one value results in proportional changes to the other two values.

Image Size Choices:

- The "Constrain Proportions" option allows you to adjust the picture size without affecting the image data, maintaining the aspect ratio.
- By selecting the "Resample Image" option, you can change the image size without compromising resolution. This is useful when printing at a specific resolution or adjusting to a resolution different from the current image specifications.

However, it's important to note that resampling may lead to a reduction in picture quality.

Image resolution also refers to the number of pixels per inch (PPI) in an image, playing a crucial role in determining the quality and size of the picture when it is printed or displayed on a screen. You can modify the resolution of your image using the Image Size dialog box. Here are key considerations to keep in mind when dealing with picture resolution:

- **Higher Resolution:** A higher resolution results in more pixels and detailed information in your picture, but it also increases the file size. High-resolution images are ideal for printing but may take longer to load or email online.
- **Lower Resolution:** Conversely, lower resolution means fewer pixels and less detail, resulting in a smaller file size. Low-resolution images work well for online or screen usage but may appear pixelated or unclear when printed.
- **Avoid Resampling:** To maintain quality and prevent unintended artifacts, avoid resampling your picture while adjusting the resolution. Resampling involves adding or subtracting pixels, potentially altering the overall appearance. Uncheck the Resample option in the Image Size dialog box to avoid this.
- **Selecting the Appropriate Resolution:** To determine the suitable resolution for your picture, consider the desired output and viewing distance. For instance, if printing on 8 × 10-inch paper with a target resolution of 300 ppi use the formula: resolution = print size × ppi. For a 300 ppi requirement, multiply 8 × 300 and 10 × 300 to achieve dimensions of 2400 × 3000 pixels. If showcasing your image on a web page with a standard

resolution of 72 ppi, use the formula: resolution = screen size × ppi. Multiply the width and height of your screen by 72 to obtain pixel measurements.

Selecting the Optimum Resolution For Printing and Onscreen Viewing

Optimal resolution for both printing and onscreen display relies on your image's size and intended purpose. Here are some general guidelines:

For onscreen viewing, like web pages, social media, or presentations, a lower resolution of 72 pixels per inch (ppi) or 96 ppi suffices. This reduces file size, ensuring faster screen loading. However, it may compromise image quality and detail, particularly if zoomed in or printed.

For printing, a higher resolution of at least 300 ppi guarantees sharp and clear output. This increases file size and print time but preserves image quality. The required resolution can vary based on the printer, paper, ink, and desired print size. Check your printer or printing service specifications for recommended resolutions.

Adjust image resolution through the Image Size dialog box. Navigate to Image > Resize > Image Size, ensure the Resample option is selected, and then input the desired resolution in the Resolution field. Adjust Width and Height accordingly. Choose an interpolation method from the drop-down menu to control how Photoshop Elements resamples the image.

Image Dimension

The image dimension denotes the width and height of your image in pixels, influencing its size on both screen and print. Modifying these dimensions can be done through either the Crop tool or the Image Size dialog box. To employ the Crop tool, navigate to Image > Crop, and adjust the cropping area by dragging the handles. Alternatively, access the Image Size dialog box via Image > Resize > Image Size, where you can input your preferred width and height in the Pixel Dimensions box.

Process of Resampling an Image

Resampling an image involves altering its pixel dimensions, influencing both file size and image quality. Follow these steps to resample an image:

1. Open the image in the Photo Editor by selecting File > Open.
2. Access the Image Size dialog box by going to Image > Resize > Image Size.
3. Ensure the Resample option at the bottom of the dialog box is checked.
4. Input the desired width and height in the Pixel Dimensions box, or opt for a preset size from the drop-down menu.
5. Choose an interpolation method from the drop-down menu adjacent to the Resample option. This method dictates how Photoshop Elements adjusts the image by adding or removing pixels. For instance, Bicubic Sharper is suitable for reducing image size, while Bicubic Smoother is effective for enlarging images.
6. Click OK to apply the changes and close the dialog box.

Getting Acquainted with Color

Color plays a crucial role in photo editing, influencing the mood, tone, and overall quality of your images. Various tools and features are at your disposal to effectively manage color:

1. **Color Picker:**
    - Easily select any color from a spectrum or input specific color values.
    - Access the Color Picker by clicking on the Foreground or Background color swatches in the Tools panel, or use the Eyedropper tool to sample a color directly from your image.
2. **Color Match Tool:**
    - Match the colors and tones of one image to another.
    - Access the Color Match tool through Enhance > Color > Color Match. Choose a source image from presets or your photos, and fine-tune hue, saturation, and brightness to achieve the desired match.
3. **Color Replacement Tool:**
    - Replace a specific color in your image with another color.
    - Access the Color Replacement tool by selecting the Brush tool and choosing Color Replacement from the Tool Options panel. Adjust parameters such as tolerance, blending mode, and limits for precise color replacement.
4. **Color Adjustment Tools:**
    - Utilize tools like Color Balance, Hue/Saturation, and Level adjustments.
    - Access these adjustments through Enhance > Adjust Color. Choose the desired option to modify the overall color of your

image or a selected area. Use sliders or eyedroppers to fine-tune color values according to your preferences.

Calibrating your Monitor

Calibrating your monitor involves adjusting the color and brightness settings to align with either a standard or your personal preference. This process ensures more accurate and consistent results when editing and printing photos. Various methods and tools are available for calibration, depending on your system and budget. Here are several options:

1. Utilize your operating system's built-in calibration utility. On Windows, navigate to Settings > System > Display > Advanced display settings > Display adapter properties > Color Management > Calibrate display. For Mac users, go to System Preferences > Display > Color > Calibrate. These utilities guide you through adjusting gamma, brightness, contrast, and color balance, allowing you to select a preset profile or create a custom one.
2. Employ a hardware device known as a colorimeter, such as Pantone Huey Pro, or Spyder. These devices measure your monitor's color and brightness, generating a profile. They come with accompanying software for installation and guide you through attaching the colorimeter to your monitor, conducting tests, and making adjustments. Colorimeters offer more precise and consistent results compared to built-in utilities.
3. Leverage the color settings and adjustments within Photoshop Element. While the software features tools like Color Picker, Color Match, Color Replacement, and adjustments like Color Balance, Hue/Saturation, and Levels, they are designed for modifying image

colors, not calibrating monitors. These tools can fine-tune colors after calibration through one of the aforementioned methods. Access these features via Enhance > Color or the Tools panel.

Selecting A color Workspace

A color workspace refers to a collection of color settings that impact the display and printing of your images. You can opt for a predefined color workspace from the Edit > Color Settings menu or craft your personalized workspace. Here are some of the available color workspaces:

1. **sRGB:**
    - Default color workspace for most digital cameras, scanners, monitors, and web browsers.
    - Ideal for images intended for onscreen viewing or web publishing.
2. **Adobe RGB:**
    - Wider color workspace compared to sRGB, showcasing a broader range of colors and shades.
    - Suitable for images intended for high-quality printing or professional editing.
3. **ProPhoto RGB:**
    - The broadest color workspace, displaying the most extensive range of colors and shades.
    - Challenging to manage as not all devices and applications can reproduce its full color spectrum.
    - Ideal for images intended for advanced editing or archival purposes.

To set a color workspace, follow these steps:

1. Navigate to Edit > Color Settings to access the Color Settings dialog box.
2. Choose a color workspace from the Working Spaces drop-down menu or click More Options to create a customized workspace.
3. Click OK to apply the changes and close the dialog box.

Image Resizing

When you navigate to the top menu bar in your software and select the "Image" menu, you can further refine your image dimensions by choosing "Resize" and then "Image Size." This action triggers a window to appear, providing you with the tools to customize the size of your image.

Within the "Image Size" window, you'll find the option to specify the desired dimensions under the section labeled "Document Size." This is where you can precisely determine how you want the image to be sized. It's worth noting that the proportions of your image will be maintained, ensuring that the original aspect ratio remains intact.

For example, as you modify the Width value, the Height will automatically adjust proportionally, preserving the original relationship between the two dimensions. This feature is particularly useful because it prevents distortion or skewing of the image, maintaining its visual integrity even as you make adjustments.

In essence, the "Image Size" dialog box provides a user-friendly interface for you to control the dimensions of your image, offering flexibility while ensuring that the aspect ratio remains consistent throughout any resizing operations. This enables you to tailor the image to your specific requirements while preserving its original visual characteristics.

About Monitor Resolution

The resolution of your monitor is determined by its pixel dimensions. For instance, if your display resolution is configured at 1600 x 1200 and your picture shares the same pixel dimensions, the photo will completely cover the screen when viewed at 100%. The onscreen appearance of an image is influenced by a combination of factors, including the pixel dimensions of the picture, the display size, and the monitor resolution setting. In Photoshop Elements, you have the flexibility to adjust the onscreen magnification of the picture, facilitating the handling of photos with varying pixel sizes.

When preparing photographs for onscreen presentation, it's important to take into account the lowest monitor resolution on which your photo is likely to be viewed. This consideration ensures that your images maintain visual appeal and clarity across a range of display devices with varying resolutions.

Monitor resolution refers to the number of pixels that your display can showcase both horizontally and vertically. This parameter significantly impacts the visual presentation of your images on the screen and also determines the available workspace.

The advantages of a higher monitor resolution are apparent—more pixels contribute to sharper and clearer images. However, it's important to acknowledge the trade-off involved. A higher resolution results in smaller icons, text, and interface elements, potentially making them more challenging to perceive and navigate. Striking a balance between resolution and usability becomes crucial, allowing you to align the display with your preferences and practical needs.

To modify your monitor resolution in Windows, follow these steps:

1. Right-click on your desktop and choose Display settings.
2. Under Scale and layout, adjust the size of text, apps, and other items.
3. In the Resolution section, select a different resolution from the drop-down menu. The recommended resolution matches your monitor's native resolution, representing its highest supported resolution.
4. Click Apply to save your changes.

For macOS users, the steps are as follows:

1. Click the Apple menu and go to System Preferences.
2. Choose Displays.
3. Under Display, select a different resolution from the Scaled options. The default resolution aligns with your monitor's native resolution.
4. Optionally, check the box for Larger Text or More Space to adjust the size of text and other items.
5. Click OK to save your changes.

In Photoshop Elements 2024, altering your monitor resolution impacts how your images are displayed and the available workspace. To achieve optimal results, use a monitor resolution compatible with your image resolution. For instance, when working with high-resolution images (e.g., 300 ppi or more), a high-resolution monitor, such as 1920 x 1080 pixels or higher, allows for detailed image viewing and provides ample room for editing.

Display the image size of an open File

Click and hold on to the file information box located at the bottom of the document. This box displays key details such as picture resolution (ppi), the number of color channels, and the width and height of the image in pixels. Additionally, the unit of measurement currently selected for the rulers is presented within this information box.

View the Print size on the Screen

1. Select Print Size from the View menu.
2. In the Tool Options menu, opt for the Zoom or Hand tool, and subsequently, click on Print Size.

When configured in the Document Size section of the Image Size dialog box, the image's magnification is adjusted to represent its approximate printed size. Keep in mind that the onscreen print size is influenced by the dimensions and resolution of your display.

Change print Dimensions and Resolution without Resampling

If you intend to send the picture to a print shop with specific quality requirements, you may need to make adjustments to the print dimensions and resolution.

However, if you are printing directly from Photoshop Elements, this step is unnecessary. Photoshop Elements automatically applies the appropriate picture resolution when selecting a size in the Print dialog box.

To adjust the print dimensions and resolution, follow these steps:

1. Select Image > Resize > Dimensions.
2. Ensure that the Resample Image option is turned off. With this option selected, you can adjust the print size and resolution without changing the overall pixel count in the image.

3. Choose Constrain Proportions to maintain the aspect ratio. When adjusting the height, the width is automatically updated accordingly.
4. Modify the height and width settings under Document Size. Optionally, select a different unit of measurement.
5. Adjust the value for Resolution. Optionally, choose a different unit of measurement.
6. Click OK to apply the changes.

Resample an Image

Resampling refers to the process of changing an image's pixel dimensions, impacting both its screen size and the quality of its printed output, specifically the resolution and dimensions for printing. It's important to note that resampling can lead to a reduction in image quality. Downsampling, or reducing the number of pixels, results in the loss of information, causing a decrease in sharpness and detail. Conversely, upsampling, or increasing the pixel count, introduces new pixels based on the color values of existing ones.

To avoid the need for up-sampling, it is recommended to scan or create the picture at the resolution required for your printer or output device. If you want to preview how changes in pixel dimensions will appear onscreen or in print proofs at various resolutions, consider resampling a copy of your file.

Follow these steps to resample and adjust pixel dimensions:

1. Select Image > Resize > Dimensions.
2. After choosing Resample Image, select an interpolation technique:
    - Fastest Neighbor: Less accurate but recommended for maintaining sharp edges in drawings with non-anti-aliased edges. This may result in jagged edges.

- Medium-quality bilinear.
- Bicubic: Slower but achieves smoother tonal gradations.
- Bicubic Smoother: Ideal for expanding photos.
- Sharper in Bicubic Form: Recommended when shrinking an image's size to maintain details, although it may oversharpen certain areas.

3. Choose Constrain Proportions to preserve the aspect ratio. Adjusting the height will automatically update the width.
4. Enter the Width and Height values in Pixel Dimensions. Select Percent as the unit of measurement for inputting percentages of the existing dimensions.
5. The image's new file size is displayed next to Pixel Dimensions, with the previous file size included in parentheses.
6. To complete the process of resampling and altering pixel dimensions, click OK.

MAXIMUM IMAGE SIZE LIMITS IN PHOTOSHOP ELEMENTS

Maximum image size limit in the Editor

In Photoshop Elements, the Editor imposes a maximum limitation on the dimensions of an image, restricting it to 30,000 pixels by 30,000 pixels. This means that you cannot open or create an image in the Editor if it surpasses this predefined limit. The restriction is in place to manage the performance and processing capabilities of the software, ensuring a smooth and efficient user experience.

The 30,000-pixel limit applies both to the width and height of the image, meaning that the total number of pixels in any direction should not exceed this threshold. This constraint is designed to balance the software's functionality with practical considerations, preventing potential issues related to system performance, memory usage, and overall responsiveness when working with large images.

Therefore, when working within the Photoshop Elements Editor, it is essential to be mindful of this limitation and consider resizing or cropping images that exceed the maximum dimensions to ensure compatibility with the software's capabilities. This ensures that users can effectively and efficiently manipulate and edit images without encountering performance issues associated with extremely large dimensions.

Maximum image size Limit in the Organizer

The maximum size of an image may be constrained by Photoshop Elements' Organizer, and this restriction is contingent on the amount of installed RAM in your machine. This limitation is implemented to prevent Photoshop Elements from attempting to utilize excessive RAM, which could lead to application slowdowns or perceived freezes, especially when working with exceptionally large photos.

If an image surpasses the allowed size, you can still import it into an Organizer catalog. However, the Organizer won't generate a thumbnail for it during import or display it in slideshows or other productions. Moreover, attempting to print the picture will result in an error notice in the Organizer, stating "Unable to print [filename], Adobe Photoshop Elements will skip printing this file." Nevertheless, the image can be viewed and edited in the Editor by selecting Edit > Go To Full Edit, as long as it adheres to the Editor's maximum image size of 30,000 by 30,000 pixels.

Refer to the table below for the maximum image dimensions corresponding to the quantity of installed RAM:

To determine the dimensions of an image in pixels, open it in

RAM Installed	Image Dimensions Limit
512 MB or less	18,874,368 pixels, or 18 megapixels
Between 512 MB and 1 GB	37,748,736 pixels, or 36 megapixels
Between 1 and 2 GB	56,623,104 pixels, or 54 megapixels
Over 2 GB	75,497,472 pixels, or 72 megapixels

Photoshop Elements Editor and navigate to Image > Resize > Image Size. Note that the provided limit values are also expressed in megapixels, where one megapixel equals 1,048,576 pixels or 1024 × 1024 pixels.

How to override the limit in the Organizer

To surpass the Organizer's maximum picture size restriction, you have the option to add a key value to the Windows registry. This allows access to larger photos than typically permitted based on the available RAM in your machine. While adding this key generally does not have adverse effects on Photoshop Elements, it's important to note that dealing with very large photographs in the Organizer may lead to lag or apparent freezing.

Please be aware that modifying the Windows registry involves editing critical system and application data and is not supported by Adobe. Refer to the Windows documentation or contact Microsoft Technical

Support for detailed information on using the Windows Registry Editor.

Important: Before proceeding, create a backup copy of the registry.

Follow these steps to exceed the Organizer's maximum picture size restriction:

1. Exit the Organizer.
2. Select "Run" from the Start menu.
3. Enter "regedit" in the Open field and click OK.
4. Navigate to the left side and select:
   - For 64-bit operating systems: **Organizer\X.0\Organizer** in **Computer\HKEY_LOCAL_MACHINE\SOFTWARE\Adobe\Elements**
5. In the left pane, highlight the "Organizer" folder.
6. Select **Edit > New > DWORD Value** and enter "MaxImageSize" as the new value.
7. Highlight the "MaxImageSize" DWORD value, then select **Edit > Modify**.
8. Choose "Decimal" as the Base option.
9. Enter the new maximum picture size in pixels in the Value Data box. For example, if you want to set the limit to 58 megapixels, enter 60817408. (Multiply the result by 1024 × 1024 to get a megapixel value in pixels.)
10. Click OK.
11. Close the registry.
12. To display thumbnails, remove any previously imported photos that exceeded the limit from the catalog and import them again

Canvas Resizing

Utilize the "Canvas Size" tool to expand or reduce the workspace surrounding the actual picture file. This command not only enables you to add or subtract workspace but also facilitates picture cropping by adjusting the canvas size.

To access this command, select "Image | Resize | Canvas Size..." from the menu bar. In the dialog box that appears, input the desired width in the "Width:" text box, and select the preferred unit of measurement from the adjacent drop-down menu. Similarly, input the desired height in the "Height:" text box and choose the unit of measurement from the drop-down menu next to it. If you opt for the "Relative" option, you can re-enter numbers and units, modifying the canvas size proportionally to its current dimensions.

CHAPTER FIVE

EXPLORING PHOTO EDITOR

Examining the Photo Editor

Presenting Photoshop Elements 2024, an advanced but approachable photo-editing program aimed at novices that replicate many of the potent tools and features of Adobe Photoshop. You can easily improve, retouch, and change your images using our cutting-edge platform to get results that seem professional.

To begin your picture editing adventure, open the Picture Editor from the Home Screen. Three different modes—Quick, Guided, and Advanced—will be shown to you based on your preferences and ability level. To meet your editing requirements, each mode provides a different combination of complexity and flexibility.

Quick Mode: Designed with ease of use in mind, Quick Mode allows you to make simple edits to your photographs. This covers standard operations like resizing, rotating, cropping, and filter application. With features like color matching, auto selection, and a variety of creative styles, the Quick Actions panel serves as a handy center for one-click modifications.

Guided Mode: Providing detailed instructions for a wide range of editing tasks, Guided mode is ideal for those looking for organized assistance. Adding text, eliminating items, changing backdrops, and making complex picture collages are all made easy using the Guided mode. To choose the ideal direction for their project, users may either go through different categories or do a particular edit search.

Advanced Mode: This mode provides access to an extensive range of potent editing tools for those seeking ultimate control and adaptability. Explore the realm of gradients, brushes, layers, and masks to make complex modifications that go beyond the fundamentals. Expert users may also edit raw files by using the Adobe Camera Raw dialog, which raises the editing experience to a professional level.

Photoshop Elements 2024 is a flexible toolbox that accommodates users of various skill levels, going beyond simple picture editing. This program offers a smooth and rewarding experience, regardless of your level of expertise with picture editing—whether you're a novice looking to dive in or an experienced user looking for an easier-to-use interface. So, use Photoshop Elements 2024 to start your creative adventure and realize the full potential of your images.

Studying Photo Editor Image Window

This tool gives you several options for viewing, zooming, panning, and rotating your photographs. To get you going, follow these steps:

1. **Launch Photoshop Elements**: Open the software and select the Photo Editor option from the main menu.
2. **Choose Editing Mode:** Within the Photo Editor, you have three modes to choose from: Quick, Guided, and Expert. Each mode offers a distinct set of tools and options for editing. Navigate between modes by clicking on the tabs at the top of the window.
3. **Open Your Image:** To open an image, click on the "Open" button in the toolbar or go to File > Open. Alternatively, you can drag and drop an image from your computer or another application into the Photo Editor window.

4. **Image Navigation:** Once your image is open, it appears in the Image Window at the center of the screen. Use the Zoom tool or the Hand tool to adjust the size and position of the image. Employ keyboard shortcuts like Ctrl/Cmd + and Ctrl/Cmd - for zooming and arrow keys for panning.
5. **Rotate Your Image:** Utilize the Rotate tool in the toolbar or go to Image > Rotate to adjust the orientation of your image. Rotate by 90 degrees clockwise or counterclockwise, or choose any custom angle. Additionally, flip the image horizontally or vertically for further adjustments.
6. **Fit Screen:** To fit the image to the screen, double-click the Hand tool in the toolbox, click the Fit Screen button in the Tool Options bar, or right-click the image and choose Fit On Screen.
7. **Full-Screen Mode:** Enter full-screen mode by pressing F11 on your keyboard or going to View > Full Screen. Exit full-screen mode by pressing F11 again or pressing Esc.
8. Add Text to Your Image: Switch to Guided mode and select the Add Text guided edit card to incorporate text into your image. This feature guides you through the steps to create and customize text, enhancing your creative possibilities.

The image viewing and editing capabilities of Photoshop Elements empower users with an intuitive and comprehensive toolkit. Whether you're a novice or an experienced editor, these steps ensure that you can navigate, enhance, and personalize your images with ease and precision. Dive into the world of creative expression with Photoshop Elements 2024's powerful features.

Revealing the Potency of Contextual Menus

Contextual menus serve as dynamic shortcuts that swiftly emerge when you right-click on different components of the Photoshop Elements interface. Designed to offer immediate access to commands and options customized to the selected tool, layer, panel, or image area, these menus are indispensable for streamlining tasks and optimizing workflow efficiency. By facilitating the quick execution of common actions without the need to switch tools or navigate intricate menus, contextual menus enhance the overall editing experience.

Explore the diversity of contextual menus within Photoshop Elements, with its specific functionalities:

1. **Layer Contextual Menu:**
    - Duplicate, delete, rename, merge, or convert layers.
    - Adjust layer attributes such as blending mode, opacity, and style.
2. **Tool Contextual Menu:**
    - Modify settings, options, and presets of the active tool.
    - Access related tools seamlessly.
3. **Image Contextual Menu:**
    - Crop, rotate, flip, resize, or transform the image.
    - Apply filters, adjustments, or effects effortlessly.
4. **Panel Contextual Menu:**
    - Customize the appearance and behavior of panels.
    - Hide, dock, group, or collapse panels as needed.

To unveil contextual menus in Photoshop Elements, simply right-click on the desired area, prompting a menu to appear with relevant commands and options. Choose the desired action or click outside the menu to cancel. Additionally, keyboard shortcuts offer a convenient alternative for accessing specific contextual menus, such as Ctrl/Cmd + click for the Layer menu or Shift + click for the Tool menu.

Contextual menus stand as a formidable feature, empowering users to edit photos with greater speed and ease. By harnessing these menus strategically, users can navigate the intricacies of the interface seamlessly, making image editing a more intuitive and efficient process.

Examining Photo Editor Tools

The Photo Editor Tools in Photoshop Elements are a whole collection of icons that are located on the left side of the screen and are only available in Photo Editor mode. These are multipurpose tools that let users do a lot of different kinds of editing on their photos. From simple operations like cropping and resizing to more complex ones like choosing, painting, drawing, erasing, cloning, and healing, these tools let users do everything.

Each tool comes equipped with its unique options and settings, conveniently adjustable through the Tool Options bar situated at the bottom of the screen. Furthermore, users can delve deeper into the capabilities of each tool by exploring different modes and presets accessible through a dropdown menu, initiated by clicking the arrow next to the tool icon in the toolbox.

Among the new and enhanced tools introduced in Photoshop Elements are:

1. **Object Selection Tool:**
    - Swiftly selects objects in images using a rectangle or lasso, powered by artificial intelligence for refined selections.
2. **Refine Selection Brush Tool:**

- Fine-tune selections with precision by adding or subtracting areas using a brush.
- Features an option for automatic edge detection, ensuring smoother and more accurate selections.

3. **Pattern Brush Tool:**
    - Empowers users to paint with patterns on images, offering a variety of preset patterns or the ability to create custom patterns from existing photos.
4. **Shape Tool:**
    - Allows users to draw various shapes on images, including rectangles, circles, stars, polygons, and more.
    - Customization options include adjusting the shape's fill, stroke, and style.

To maximize the potential of these tools, users can seamlessly navigate through the Tool Options bar, tailoring their editing experience to specific project requirements. Whether you're a novice or an experienced editor, the intuitive nature of these tools combined with advanced features like artificial intelligence-powered selection make Photoshop Elements 2024 a powerhouse for creative image editing. Explore the possibilities and elevate your editing capabilities with these new and improved tools.

View Group Tools

In Photoshop Elements, group tools refer to tools that offer a range of functionalities under a single tool icon within the Tools panel. These tools are designed to streamline the user interface by consolidating related functions, providing quick access to various options without cluttering the workspace. To access the different tools within a group, users have two convenient methods:

1. **Click and Hold:** By clicking and holding on the tool icon, a dropdown menu appears, unveiling the additional tools grouped under the selected icon. Users can then hover over the desired tool and release the mouse button to activate it. For instance, the rectangular marquee tool serves as a prime example of a group tool, encompassing options like the elliptical marquee tool, single-row marquee tool, and single-column marquee tool.

2. **Right-Click and Select:** Another method involves a right-click on the tool icon. Upon right-clicking, a pop-up menu emerges, presenting a list of the available tools within the group. Users can then choose the specific tool they wish to employ from this menu. This intuitive approach ensures easy navigation and swift access to the diverse range of tools encapsulated within a group.

These group tools not only optimize the workspace by condensing related functionalities but also enhance the overall user experience by providing a seamless means of selecting and utilizing various tools as per the editing requirements. As users become familiar with the grouping system, they gain efficiency in their workflows, contributing to a more fluid and productive editing process within Photoshop Elements.

Select Group Tools

In the realm of photo editing, a selection serves as a defined area within an image that bestows the power of editability upon the chosen region. This allows for nuanced adjustments, such as brightening specific segments of a photo without affecting the entirety. Selections can be crafted using either dedicated selection tools or specialized selection commands, creating a designated editable zone encapsulated by a selection border. Notably, this border, though visible, can be concealed for a clearer view of the image.

Adobe Photoshop Elements offers an array of selection tools tailored to diverse selection needs. For instance, the Elliptical Marquee tool excels in selecting circular and elliptical areas, while the Magic Wand tool proves adept at swiftly selecting regions with similar colors in a single click. For more intricate selections, the Lasso tools come into play, providing the flexibility to create complex shapes with precision. Moreover, Photoshop Elements extends the capability to refine selections through features like feathering and anti-aliasing. Feathering introduces a gradual transition along the edges of a selection, allowing for smoother and more natural blends. On the other hand, anti-aliasing enhances the overall quality of the selection by smoothing the jagged edges, especially beneficial when working with the Elliptical Marquee tool.

It's crucial to note that pixels within the selection border can be altered, copied, or deleted, offering a targeted approach to photo editing. However, any adjustments outside the selection border remain inaccessible until the selection is deselected.

In essence, the robust suite of selection tools in Adobe Photoshop Elements empowers users to tailor their editing process according to the intricacy of their projects, ensuring precision, flexibility, and efficiency in crafting compelling visual narratives.

Use selection tools

The selection tools are essential for identifying and modifying certain regions of a picture, and they are located in Adobe Photoshop

Elements' Tools panel. This panel, which is usually oriented to the left of the screen by default, serves as a primary hub for accessing a range of tools necessary for various editing activities.

But it's important to remember that Photoshop Elements requires that you be in advanced mode for the selection tools to be visible. Users must click on advanced mode to access the complete range of selection tools and fully use them. This will show an extensive toolset that is specifically tailored to meet complex selection requirements.

Adobe's dedication to giving customers an intuitive but robust interface is shown by the well-placed selection tools in the Tools panel and the need to be in Advanced mode. By ensuring that users can easily access and use these tools when required, this method improves their capacity to make accurate and personalized decisions for efficient picture editing in Photoshop Elements.

Utilize the Power of Rectangular and Elliptical Marquee Tools in Photoshop Elements:

The Rectangular and Elliptical Marquee tools stand as indispensable assets for crafting precise selection borders within Adobe Photoshop Elements. Whether you intend to define a square or rectangular area or encircle an object with a round or elliptical border, these tools offer unparalleled flexibility.

Rectangular and Elliptical Marquee Tools Overview: Rectangular and Elliptical Marquee tool options are integral components of the selection arsenal, each serving distinct purposes in the photo editing journey. The toolbox includes:

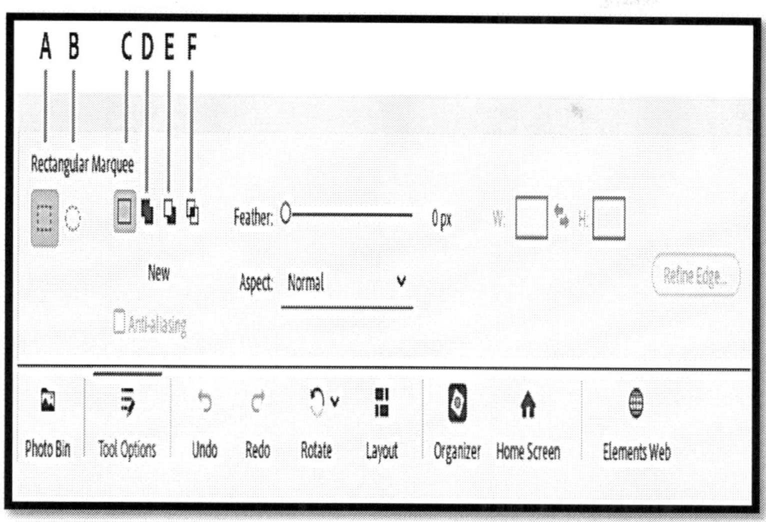

- A. Rectangular Marquee tool
- B. Elliptical Marquee tool
- C. New selection
- D. Add to the selection
- E. Subtract from selection
- F. Intersect with selection

Mastering the Selection Process:

1. **Tool Selection:** Begin by selecting the desired marquee tool – Rectangular (A) or Elliptical (B) – from the toolbox.
2. **Tool Options Configuration:** Navigate to the Tool Options bar to fine-tune your marquee tool experience. Here, you can:
    - Specify whether to create a new selection, add to a selection, subtract from a selection, or intersect with other selections.
    - Introduce a feather value to soften the selection border for seamless integration with the surrounding area.
    - Opt for anti-aliasing (specific to the Elliptical Marquee tool) to achieve smoother edges.
    - Choose from the Mode pop-up menu:

- **Normal:** Visually set the size and proportions of the selection border.
- **Fixed Ratio:** Establish a specific width-to-height ratio for the selection border.
- **Fixed Size:** Specify the height and width of the marquee.

3. **Drag and Constrain:** With your tool settings in place, drag over the target area for selection. Hold down the Shift key during the drag to constrain the selection marquee to a perfect square or circle.
4. **Additional Techniques:**
   - **Center Drag:** Hold down Alt (Windows) or Option (Mac OS) after initiating the drag to move the marquee from the center.
   - **Repositioning:** Hold down the spacebar while dragging with the selection tool to reposition the selection border. Release the spacebar once the border is in the desired area.
5. **Refine for Precision:** Further enhance your selection by clicking on "Refine Edge," enabling you to make intricate adjustments and achieve a more precise selection. Explore the refinement options to put the edges according to your vision.

Use the Lasso tool

The Lasso tool emerges as a dynamic instrument within Adobe Photoshop Elements, offering the freedom to craft freehand selection borders with unparalleled precision. Elevate your photo editing experience by mastering the intricacies of this tool.

Lasso Tool Unveiled: The Lasso tool encompasses various options and functionalities designed to cater to diverse selection needs. Navigate the toolbox, which includes:

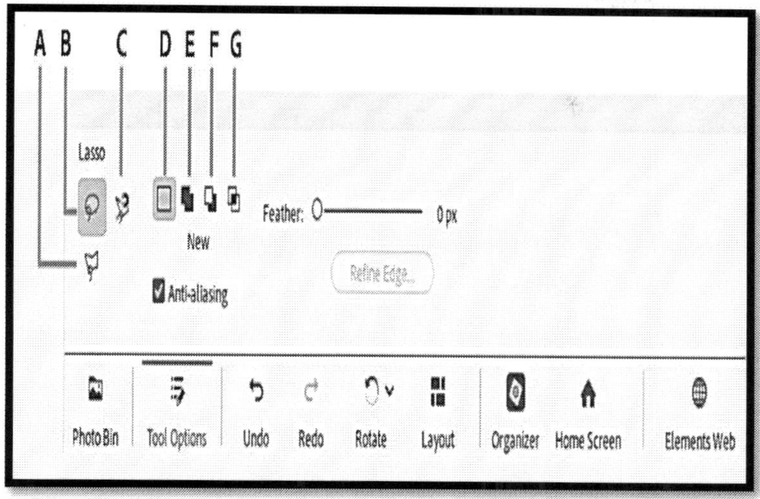

- A. Lasso tool
- B. Polygonal Lasso tool
- C. Magnetic Lasso tool
- D. New selection
- E. Add to selection
- F. Subtract from selection
- G. Intersect with selection

Steps to Utilize the Lasso Tool:

1. **Tool Selection:** Commence by selecting the Lasso tool (A) from the toolbox, setting the stage for freehand selection precision.
2. **Tool Options Configuration:** Explore the Tool Options bar to customize your Lasso tool experience. Here, you can:
   - Specify the type of selection to create: new, add to an existing selection, subtract from a selection, or intersect with other selections.
   - Introduce a feather value to soften the selection border for seamless integration with the surrounding area.

- Opt for anti-aliased edges to achieve a smoother selection border.

3. **Freehand Selection:** With your tool options defined, initiate the freehand selection process. Drag the cursor to draw a selection border according to your creative vision.
4. **Advanced Selection Techniques:**
   - **Add to Selection:** Release the mouse button, then press Shift and, when the pointer changes, drag to add to the selection.
   - **Subtract from Selection:** Release the mouse button, then press Alt (Option in Mac OS), and when the pointer changes, drag to subtract from the selection.
   - **Add Straight-Edge Segments*:*** Hold the mouse button and press Alt (Option in Mac OS), then release the mouse button. When the pointer changes, click where you want to position the end of the segment.
5. **Closing the Selection:** To finalize your freehand selection, release the mouse button. A straight selection segment is drawn from the release point to the starting point, closing the selection border.
6. **Refine for Precision:** Click on "Refine Edge" to delve into additional adjustments, refining the selection and enhancing its precision. Unleash the potential to achieve intricate selections that align seamlessly with your creative vision.

Use the Polygonal Lasso tool

One useful tool in Adobe Photoshop Elements is the Polygonal Lasso tool, which allows you to draw straight lines to create a well-defined selection boundary. As we examine the many features and methods this advanced program offers, you will be able to edit photos more skillfully.

Demystifying the Polygonal Lasso Tool: Discover the intricacies of the Polygonal Lasso tool, equipped with options and features denoted by:

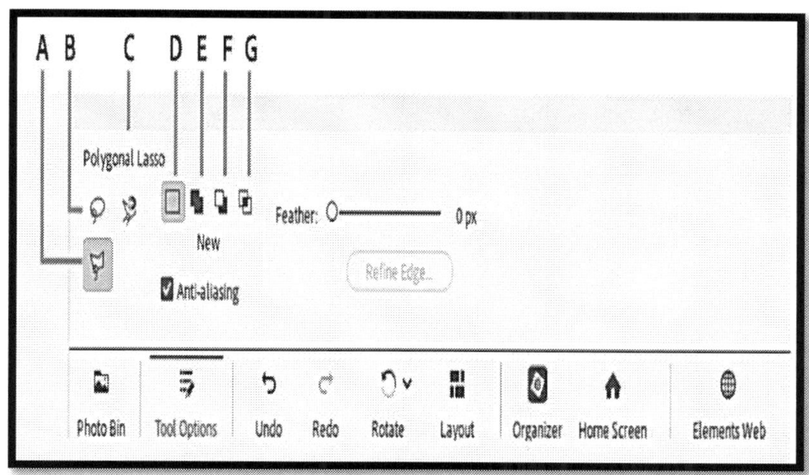

- A. Lasso tool
- B. Polygonal Lasso tool
- C. Magnetic Lasso tool
- D. New selection
- E. Add to selection
- F. Subtract from selection
- G. Intersect with selection

Step-by-Step Guide to Utilizing the Polygonal Lasso Tool:

1. **Tool Selection:** Initiate the selection process by choosing the Polygonal Lasso tool (B) from the toolbox, setting the stage for creating precise straight-edged segments.
2. **Tool Options Configuration:** Customize your Polygonal Lasso tool experience by exploring the Tool Options bar, where you can:

- Determine the type of selection to create: new, add to an existing selection, subtract from a selection, or intersect with other selections.
- Introduce a feather value to seamlessly blend the selection border with the surrounding area.
- Opt for anti-aliased edges to achieve a smooth and refined selection border.

3. **Segment Creation:** With your tool options configured, embark on segment creation. Click where you want the first straight segment to begin, and click a second time where you want the segment to end, signaling the commencement of the next one. Continue this process to fashion intricate and straight-edged segments as needed.
4. **Error Correction:** Rectify mistakes by pressing the Delete key to erase segments. Switch seamlessly between creating straight-edge segments and drawing freehand by pressing Alt (Option in Mac OS).
5. **Closing the Selection:** Bring your selection to completion by adopting one of the following approaches:
   - Position the pointer over the starting point and click. A closed circle indicates alignment with the starting point.
   - If the pointer isn't directly over the starting point, opt for a double-click or Ctrl-click (Command-click in Mac OS). A straight selection segment connects your pointer to the starting point, finalizing the selection border.
6. **Precision Refinement:** Elevate the precision of your selection by clicking on "Refine Edge." This feature opens avenues for additional

adjustments, ensuring a selection that aligns seamlessly with your creative vision.

Use the Magnetic Lasso tool

Explore the realm of accurate choices with Adobe Photoshop Elements' feature-rich Magnetic Lasso tool, which sticks to object edges flawlessly to provide exact boundaries for your artistic pursuits. Make use of this sophisticated tool's subtleties and powers to enhance your photo-editing experience.

Understanding the Magnetic Lasso Tool: The Magnetic Lasso tool stands out as a sophisticated solution for drawing selection borders that intelligently adhere to the contours of objects within your photo. Its automatic snapping feature to object edges simplifies the process, making it particularly effective for swiftly selecting objects against complex backgrounds with high-contrast elements.

Navigating the Magnetic Lasso Tool Interface: Regarding the annotations shown by the tool settings below**:**

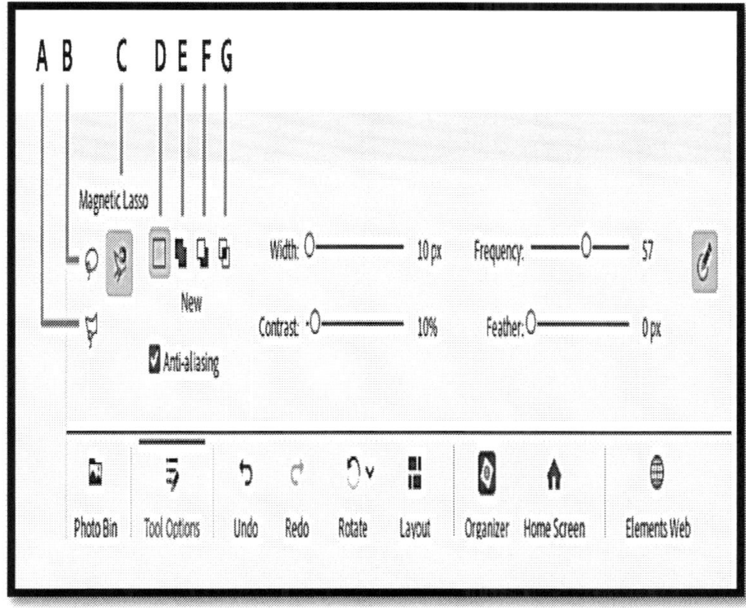

- A. Lasso tool
- B. Polygonal Lasso tool
- C. Magnetic Lasso tool
- D. New selection
- E. Add to selection
- F. Subtract from selection
- G. Intersect with selection

Step-by-Step Guide to Utilizing the Magnetic Lasso Tool:

1. **Tool Selection:** Kickstart your precision selection journey by selecting the Magnetic Lasso tool (C) from the toolbox.
2. **Switching Tools:** Seamlessly transition between the Magnetic Lasso and other lasso tools with the following commands:
   - Activate the Lasso tool by pressing Alt (Option in Mac OS) and dragging.
   - Activate the Polygonal Lasso tool by pressing Alt (Option in Mac OS) and clicking.
3. **Tool Options Customization:** Tailor your Magnetic Lasso tool experience with these customizable options found in the Tool Options bar:
   - Specify the type of selection: new, add to an existing selection, subtract from a selection, or intersect with other selections.
   - Introduce a feather value for a seamlessly blending selection border.
   - Opt for anti-aliased edges for a smooth finish.
   - Define the area of edge detection by entering a pixel value between 1 and 256.

4. **Fine-Tuning Sensitivity:** Refine the tool's performance by adjusting:
   - Magnetic Lasso pointer appearance by pressing the Caps Lock key.
   - Edge Contrast between 1% and 100%, determining sensitivity to contrasting edges.
   - Frequency for fastening points, with higher values anchoring the selection border more quickly.
5. **Adding Selection Segments:** Incorporate segments into your selection border through various methods:
   - Click points along the edge.
   - Drag along the edge while pressing the mouse button.
6. **Snap to Edge:** Witness the selection border intelligently snapping to the edge of the photo. If needed, manually add points by clicking once.
7. **Closing the Selection Border:** Conclude your selection process by adopting one of these closure methods:
   - Manually close the border by dragging back over the starting point and clicking.
   - Close the border with a freehand magnetic segment by double-clicking or pressing Enter.
   - Close the border with a straight segment by double-clicking while pressing Alt (Option in Mac OS).

Use the Magic Wand tool

The Magic Wand tool in Adobe Photoshop Elements is a user-friendly function that allows you to choose pixels within a specific range with ease. Use it to start your adventure through pixel selection. Make use of the many features and options this program offers to refine your editing skills and get unmatched creative freedom.

Exploring the Magic Wand Tool: One particularly useful tool for picking pixels based on color similarity is the Magic Wand tool. It offers a quick and effective way to isolate a blue sky or any other region with a consistent color scheme.

Navigating the Magic Wand Tool Interface: Check out the annotations below, indicated by the tool options:

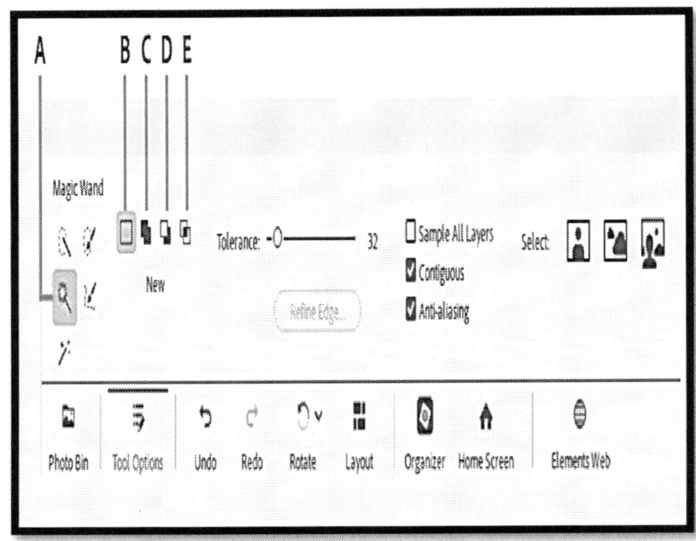

- A. Magic Wand tool
- B. New selection
- C. Add to the selection
- D. Subtract from selection
- E. Intersect with selection

Step-by-Step Guide to Utilizing the Magic Wand Tool:

1. Selection: Initiate your pixel selection process by selecting the Magic Wand tool (A) from the toolbox.

2. Tool Options Customization: Put your Magic Wand tool experience with these customizable options found in the Tool Options bar:

3. Tolerance: Define the color range by entering a value between 0 and 255. Opt for a lower value for precise color selection or a higher value for a broader range.

4. Anti-aliased: Choose to have a smooth selection edge by selecting anti-aliased.

5. Contiguous: Specify whether to select only adjacent areas with the same colors. Deselecting allows the selection of similar colors throughout the entire photo.

6 Sample All Layers: Decide whether the Magic Wand tool should consider colors from all visible layers or only the active layer.

7. Color Selection: Click on the color in the photo that you wish to select based on the specified color range.

8. Selection Refinement: Fine-tune your selection using the following commands:

- To add to the selection, Shift+click on unselected areas.
- To remove an area from the selection, press Alt (Option in Mac OS) and click on the area to be removed.

9. Further Adjustment: Click on "Refine Edge" to delve deeper into adjustments and enhance the precision of your selection. Discover how to refine the edges for a polished outcome.

Use the Quick Selection tool

Improve your editing skills with Adobe Photoshop Elements' clever Quick Selection Brush tool, which lets you quickly choose images based on similarities in texture and color. Explore every aspect of this tool, which is designed to create selections quickly and intuitively while offering a smooth editing experience.

Understanding the Quick Selection Brush Tool:

The Quick Selection tool operates by interpreting color and texture similarities, requiring only a simple click or click-drag to initiate the selection process. The tool automatically generates a border, eliminating the need for pinpoint accuracy during the initial selection. Note: Explore the capabilities of the Smart Brush tool, which not only creates selections akin to the Quick Selection tool but also simultaneously applies color or tonal adjustments.

Quick Selection Brush Tool Interface: Please review the annotations below, which are indicated by the tool choices:

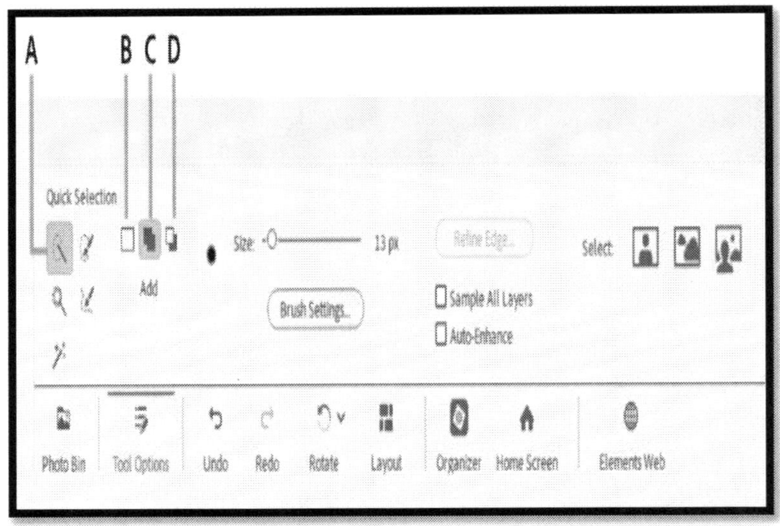

- **A.** Quick Selection tool
- B. New selection
- C. Add to the selection
- D. Subtract from selection

Effortless Selection Process:

1. **Tool Selection:** Choose the Quick Selection Brush tool to commence your selection journey.
2. **Tool Options Customization:**
   - **New Selection:** Opt for drawing a new selection, the default option.
   - **Add To Selection:** Choose to add to an existing selection.
   - **Subtract From Selection:** Utilize this option to subtract from an existing selection, available after an initial selection.
3. **Brush Customization:** In the Tool Options bar, select a suitable brush from the Brush Picker. For extensive areas, opt for a larger brush, while precision demands a smaller size.
4. **Selection Initiation:** Click or click-drag over the area encompassing the color range of the desired object, then release the mouse button to witness the automatic appearance of the selection border.
5. **Refinement Techniques:**
   - Adding to the Selection: Click the "Add to Selection" button in the options bar, then click or click-drag across the area to be added.
   - Subtracting from the Selection: Click the "Subtract from Selection" button in the options bar, then click or click-drag across the area to be subtracted.
   - Starting a New Selection: Click the "New Selection" button in the options bar to initiate a new selection area.
6. **Selection Refinement:** Click on "Refine Edge" for advanced adjustments, enhancing the precision of your selection. Explore the refinements available to polish the selection edges seamlessly.

Use the Selection Brush tool

The Selection Brush tool is a very adaptable tool with two functions. Using a semiopaque overlay in Mask mode, you may apply strokes to regions to be excluded, or you can paint over the required area in Selection mode to create selections.

Discover the possibilities of the Selection Brush tool, which can expertly refine choices. Select a mask mode for exclusion or selection mode for inclusion to provide a more sophisticated method of selection refining.

Selection Brush Tool Interface:

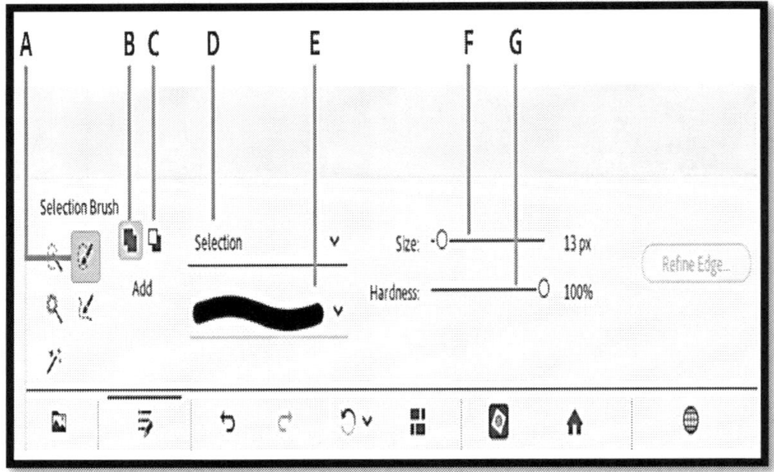

- **A**. Selection Brush
- B. Add to the selection
- C. Subtract from selection
- D. Selection pop-up
- E. Brush pop-up
- F. Brush size
- G. Hardness

Initiating the Selection Brush Journey:

1. **Tool Activation:** Select the Selection Brush tool from the toolbox. If needed, access it by clicking the Quick Selection tool and selecting the Selection Brush from the hidden tools list.
2. **Mode Configuration:** By default, the tool is set to "Add to Selection." For subtraction, click "Subtract from Selection" in the options bar.
3. **Tool Options Customization:**
   - Brush Selection: Choose a brush from the brush presets pop-up panel.
   - Brush Size: Specify the brush size according to the selection requirements.
   - Mode Selection: Choose between Selections (to add) or Mask (to subtract) from the Mode menu.
   - Brush Hardness: Set the hardness level between 1% and 100%.
4. **Visual Enhancements:** When using a soft-edged brush, switching to mask mode aids in visualizing the soft edges effectively. Adjust the overlay opacity and color to enhance visibility.
5. **Mask Mode Configuration:**
   - Overlay Opacity: Specify an overlay opacity between 1% and 100%.
   - Overlay Color: Click the Overlay Color swatch to choose a distinct color for the mask, ensuring clarity against photo colors.
6. **Selection Process:** Draw on your photo to select or deselect areas based on the chosen mode.

Fine-tuning with the Refine Selection Brush Tool: Explore the capabilities of the Refine Selection Brush tool, a companion tool that automatically detects edges, facilitating the addition or removal of areas to and from a selection. This tool streamlines the refinement process, ensuring precision in your selections.

Use the Auto Selection tool

The Auto Selection tool is a game-changer in the dynamic world of Adobe Photoshop Elements, bringing a smooth approach to choices. By automatically creating choices based on the shapes drawn around desirable items, this tool gives users more control. Because the tool is so good at interpreting the contours of chosen items, precision is less important and it may be used by people of all skill levels.

Exploring the Auto Selection Tool Interface: Navigate the Auto Selection tool with ease, utilizing the following annotated elements:

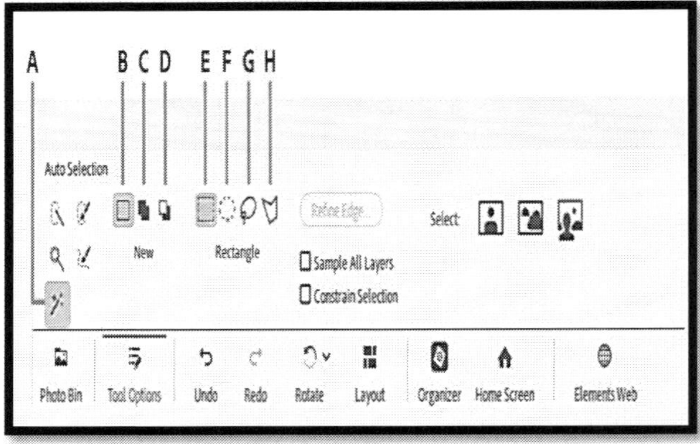

- A. Auto Selection Tool
- B. New Selection
- C. Add to Selection
- D. Subtract from Selection
- E. Rectangle
- F. Ellipse
- G. Lasso
- H. Polygon Lasso

Initiating the Auto Selection Journey:

1. **Tool Activation:** Access the Auto Selection tool in the toolbar, available in both Quick and Advanced modes.
2. **Mode Configuration:** Choose the appropriate mode from the Tool Options bar:
    - New selection: The default option for drawing a new selection.
    - Add to selection: Incorporate new elements into an existing selection.
    - Subtract from selection: Eliminate portions from an existing selection (available post-initial selection).
3. **Shape Selection:** Select one of the following shapes to draw around the object to be selected:
    - Rectangle: Ideal for drawing rectangular segments.
    - Ellipse: Tailored for drawing elliptical or circular segments.
    - Lasso: Perfect for drawing free-form segments.
    - Polygon Lasso: Well-suited for drawing straight-edged segments.
4. **Drawing the Selection:** Effortlessly draw around the desired object in the photo, letting the Auto Selection tool interpret the outlines.
5. **Refining the Selection:**
    - Adding to the Selection: Click the "Add to Selection" button in the options bar and draw across the area to include.
    - Subtracting from the Selection: Click the "Subtract from Selection" button in the options bar and draw across the area to exclude.

- Starting a New Selection: Click the "New Selection" button in the options bar and draw to specify a new selection area.

6. **Precision Refinement:** Click "Refine Edge" to delve into advanced adjustments, ensuring precision in your selection. This step opens the door to additional fine-tuning for a polished outcome.

Navigating Tips for Optimal Results: For optimal results, consider selecting one object at a time. After selecting one object, seamlessly integrate another using the "Add to Selection" option.

Enhance Group Tool

The group tool is a powerful feature that enables you to efficiently manage and manipulate multiple layers as a cohesive unit. Here are comprehensive guidelines to maximize the utility of the group tool:

Creating and Managing Groups:

1. **Creating a Group:**
    - Select the layers you want to group in the Layers panel.
    - Click the "Create a new group" icon at the bottom of the panel.
    - Alternatively, use the keyboard shortcuts Ctrl+G (Windows) or Command+G (Mac).
2. **Adding or Removing Layers:**
    - To add layers to a group, drag and drop them into the group in the Layers panel.
    - To remove layers, drag them out of the group.
    - Utilize Ctrl+Shift+G (Windows) or Command+Shift+G (Mac) to ungroup selected layers.
3. **Renaming a Group:**
    - Double-click the group name in the Layers panel to edit it.

- Alternatively, right-click the group and choose "Rename Group" from the context menu.

Applying Adjustments, Effects, and Mask

4. **Group-wide Adjustments:**
   - Select the group in the Layers panel.
   - Use the Adjustments, Effects, or Masks panel to apply adjustments, effects, or masks.
   - The changes will be applied collectively to all layers within the group.
5. **Layer Styles for Groups:**
   - Employ the Layer Style dialog box to apply styles like drop shadows, bevels, or strokes to the entire group.
   - Right-click on the group, select "Blending Options," and explore the available styles.

Enhancing Groups with Photomerge Guided Edits

6. **Accessing Photomerge Guided Edits:**
   - Navigate to guided mode and select "Photomerge" from the list of categories.
7. **Choosing Photomerge Type:**
   - Select the type of Photomerge you want to perform, such as group shot, scene cleaner, or exposure.
8. **Source Selection and Adjustment:**
   - Follow on-screen instructions to choose source groups and adjust settings.
   - This is particularly useful for creating surreal scenes, perfect group photos, or blended shots by merging multiple groups.

Draw Group Tool

The Draw Group Tool is an innovative addition to Photoshop Element 2024, facilitating the creation of shapes and paths directly on a group of layers. This feature proves invaluable for crafting customized designs, logos, icons, or text effects effortlessly. Here's a step-by-step guide on utilizing the Draw Group Tool:

1. **Selecting the Target Group:**
    - Open the Layers panel and choose the group of layers you intend to draw on. Create a new group using the "Create a new group" icon or utilize existing groups in your project.
2. **Activating the Draw Group Tool**:
    - Click on the Draw Group Tool icon located in the Tools panel, identifiable by a pencil with a group symbol. Alternatively, press Shift+D to activate the tool.
3. **Choosing Shape or Path:**
    - Access the Options bar to select the desired shape or path. Options include preset shapes like rectangles, circles, stars, polygons, or custom shapes. Opt for the Pen tool for freeform paths or the Curvature tool for smooth curves.
4. **Adjusting Shape/Path Settings:**
    - Fine-tune settings for the chosen shape or path in the Options bar. Modify fill color, stroke color, stroke width, stroke style, and other parameters. Utilize Transform controls to resize, rotate, or reposition the shape or path on the canvas.
5. **Drawing on the Canvas:**
    - Click and drag on the canvas to draw the selected shape or path onto the group of layers. Employ guides and grids for

alignment and utilize Shift, Alt, or Ctrl keys to modify the shape or path dynamically.

6. **Completing the Drawing:**
   - Release the mouse button when the drawing is complete. The shape or path is incorporated as a vector mask within the group, revealing only the parts of the group enclosed by the shape or path. The vector mask thumbnail appears next to the group name in the Layers panel.
7. **Editing the Shape/Path:**
   - To edit the shape or path, double-click the vector mask thumbnail in the Layers panel to enter Path Selection mode. Use the Path Selection Tool or Direct Selection Tool to make modifications. Employ the Properties panel to adjust fill and stroke options or the Layer Style dialog box to apply effects like drop shadow, bevel, or stroke to the entire group.

Modify Group Tools

Modifying group tools involves adjusting the settings or appearance of tools applied to a group of layers. This process allows for the customization of elements such as fill color, stroke width, layer style, shape, and vector mask. Here are various methods to modify group tools:

1. **Changing Fill Color:**
   - Select the group in the Layers panel.
   - Click the Fill icon in the Options bar.
   - Choose a fill type from the drop-down menu, such as solid color, gradient, or pattern.

- Use the Color Picker to select a custom color or the Eyedropper to sample a color from the image.

2. **Adjusting Stroke Width:**
   - Select the group in the Layers panel.
   - Click the Stroke icon in the Options bar.
   - Adjust the stroke width by dragging the slider or entering a specific value.
   - Modify stroke color, style, and alignment from the drop-down menu.
3. **Changing Layer Style:**
   - Select the group in the Layers panel.
   - Click the "fx" icon at the bottom of the panel to access Layer Styles.
   - Choose from styles like drop shadow, bevel, or stroke.
   - Adjust settings in the Layer Style dialog box.
   - Utilize the Style Settings panel to apply preset styles or create custom ones.
4. **Choosing a Different Shape or Path:**
   - Select the group in the Layers panel.
   - Click the Shape icon in the Options bar.
   - Choose from preset shapes like rectangles, circles, stars, polygons, or custom shapes.
   - Opt to draw a freeform path with the Pen tool or use the Curvature tool for smooth curves.
5. **Editing the Vector Mask:**
   - Double-click the vector mask thumbnail in the Layers panel to enter Path Selectmode.

- Use the Path Selection Tool or Direct Selection Tool to select and modify the shape or path.
- Utilize the Properties panel to adjust fill and stroke options.
- Access the Layer Style dialog box to apply styles like drop shadow, bevel, or stroke to the entire group.

Making Selections from the Tool Panels

Creating selections from the tool panels involves utilizing a variety of tools available in the Tools panel to isolate specific parts of an image. These tools enable users to modify, enhance, or isolate particular areas of an image, as well as to generate masks, layers, or shapes. Below are some of the selection tools available:

1. **Quick Selection Tool:**
    - Allows selection by dragging over an area of similar pixels.
    - Adjust brush size and hardness, and use Add or Subtract modes for refinement.
    - Utilize Refine Edge for smoothing, feathering, or expanding selections.
2. **Magic Wand Tool:**
    - Enables selection by clicking on an area of similar pixels.
    - Adjust tolerance and contiguous settings for pixel selection control.
    - Use Add or Subtract modes for further selection refinement.
3. **Lasso Tool:**
    - Creates selections by drawing a freehand outline around an area.
    - Adjust feather and anti-alias settings for smoother edges.

- Apply to Add or Subtract modes for additional selection control.

4. **Magnetic Lasso Tool:**
   - Makes selections by drawing an outline that snaps to area edges.
   - Adjust width, contrast, and frequency settings for edge detection control.
   - Use Add or Subtract modes for precise selection adjustments.
5. **Polygonal Lasso Tool:**
   - Generates selections with a straight-edged outline around an area.
   - Adjust feather and anti-alias settings for refined edges.
   - Apply to Add or Subtract modes for further selection control.
6. **Selection Brush Tool:**
   - Makes selections by painting over an area with a brush.
   - Adjust brush size, hardness, and opacity.
   - Utilize Selection or Mask modes for creating or modifying selections.
   - Apply Add or Subtract modes for fine-tuning selections.
7. **Auto Selection Tool:**
   - Enables selection by drawing a rectangle or ellipse over an area.
   - Automatically selects the most prominent object within the shape.
   - Adjust the size and shape of the selection, and use Add or Subtract modes for precision.

Making a Selection from the Tool Options

Selecting the subject, sky, or backdrop of your shot automatically with only one click is possible when you use Tool Options. The steps below can be used to execute a selection from the Tool Options:

1. Open the photo you wish to edit in the Photo Editor by selecting File > Open.
2. Choose any selection tool from the Tools panel, such as the Quick Selection tool, Lasso tool, or Magic Wand tool.
3. In the Tool Options panel situated below the image window, locate three buttons labeled Subject, Sky, and Background. Click the button corresponding to the specific area you want to select in your photo. For instance, click the Sky button if you intend to select the sky.
4. Photoshop Elements will employ Adobe Sensei AI technology to automatically select the designated area. A selection border will appear around the chosen area, which you can further refine using selection brushes or the Refine Edge tool.

Working with the Photo Editor Panel Bin

The Photo Editor Panel Bin is a versatile feature in Photoshop Element, offering easy access and management of various editing panels and tabs. Depending on your editing mode—Quick, Guided, or Expert—the Panel Bin displays different options. Here's a guide on how to navigate and customize the Photo Editor Panel Bin:

1. **Opening the Photo Editor Panel Bin:**
    - Click the Photo Editor button on the home screen.
    - Choose the desired mode: Quick, Guided, or Expert.

- The Panel Bin will appear on the right side of the workspace.

2. **Switching Between Modes:**
   - Click the Mode button at the top of the Panel Bin.
   - Choose the mode you want to work in (Quick, Guided, or Expert).
   - The Panel Bin adjusts to display relevant panels and tabs for the selected mode.
3. **Accessing Panels and Tabs:**
   - In the Panel Bin, click the icons or names of the panels and tabs you want to use.
   - For example, in Expert mode, click the Layers icon to manage photo layers or the Effects icon to apply various effects.
   - Click the More button to see a comprehensive list of available panels and tabs, selecting the desired one from the pop-up menu.
4. **Customizing the Panel Bin:**
   - Click the arrow next to the More button.
   - Select "Custom Workspace" to arrange panels and tabs in a tabbed layout.
   - Drag and drop panels and tabs to reorder, group, or dock them at the bottom of the Panel Bin.
   - Resize the Panel Bin by dragging its left edge.
   - Collapse the Panel Bin by clicking the double arrow icon at the top.

Maintaining a Relationship with Photo Bin

The Photo Bin feature facilitates the viewing and management of opened photos within the Photo Editor. It enables users to switch between images, compare them side by side, create albums, and perform various tasks. To effectively interact with the Photo Bin, consider the following guidelines:

- To toggle the Photo Bin's visibility, either click the Photo Bin button located at the bottom of the Photo Editor window or use the shortcut Ctrl+B (Windows) or Command+B (Mac).
- To add photos to the Photo Bin, either select File > Open or drag and drop photos from your computer or the organizer.
- To remove photos from the Photo Bin, right-click on a photo and choose Close, or use the shortcut Ctrl+W (Windows) or Command+W (Mac). This action closes the photo in the Photo Editor without deleting it from your computer or the organizer.
- Single-click on a photo in the Photo Bin to select it. The chosen photo will be displayed in the image window, accompanied by a blue border around its thumbnail in the Photo Bin.
- For selecting multiple photos, hold down Ctrl (Windows) or Command (Mac) while clicking on the desired photos. Alternatively, click and drag a marquee around the photos you wish to select.
- To compare photos within the Photo Bin, select two or more photos and click the Compare button at the bottom of the Photo Bin. This action opens the Compare Photos dialog box, allowing side-by-side viewing with zoom options. Additionally, use the buttons in the dialog box for rotation, cropping, or applying quick fixes to the photos.
- To create an album from the Photo Bin's contents, select the desired photos and click the Create Album button at the bottom of the Photo Bin. This opens the Create Album dialog box, where you can name the album and choose a saving location. The album will appear in the Albums panel within the organizer.

- Access additional options for photos in the Photo Bin by right-clicking on a photo and selecting from the pop-up menu. Alternatively, use the buttons at the bottom of the Photo Bin for actions such as rotation, deletion, or printing of photos.

Creating Different Views for a Photo

Exploring various edits and comparing them side by side is achieved through the creation of different views for a photo. This can be accomplished using the History panel, the Compare Photos dialog box, or the Reels feature. Here are step-by-step instructions:

Using the History Panel:

1. Open the photo in the Photo Editor via File > Open.
2. Apply edits using Expert mode tools and adjustments.
3. Navigate to Window > History to access the History panel.
4. Utilize the New Snapshot button to create a snapshot of the current photo, assigning a name and description if desired.
5. Continue editing and create additional snapshots as needed.
6. View a snapshot by clicking its name in the History panel.
7. To compare two snapshots, select them and click the Compare button at the bottom of the panel. This opens the Compare Photos dialog box for a side-by-side comparison with zoom options.

Using the Compare Photos Dialog Box:

1. Open two or more photos in the Photo Editor via File > Open.
2. Access the Compare Photos dialog box by going to Window > Images > Compare Photos.
3. Observe the photos side by side, with zoom capabilities.
4. Employ the buttons at the top of the dialog box for rotation, cropping, or quick fixes.

5. Switch between photos by clicking the Swap button at the bottom of the dialog box.
6. Close the dialog box by clicking the done button.

Using the Reels Feature:

1. Open the photo in the Photo Editor via File > Open.
2. Launch the Reels panel by going to Enhance > Reels.
3. Explore a reel showcasing various edits like black and white, vintage, or artistic.
4. Scroll through the reel and select an edit.
5. Customize the chosen edit using the sliders below the reel.
6. To create a custom edit, click the Add button at the bottom of the reel, providing a name and adjusting settings.
7. Compare two edits by selecting them and clicking the Compare button at the bottom of the reel. This opens the Compare Photos dialog box for a side-by-side comparison with zoom options.

Exploring Guided Edit Mode

Guided Edit Mode serves as a feature designed for effortlessly applying various effects and enhancements to your photos through step-by-step instructions. With a selection of 62 Guided Edits organized into six categories, namely Basics, Color, Black & White, Fun Edits, Special Edits, and Photomerge, users have a wide array of creative options. Noteworthy additions to the 2024 version include new Guided Edits like Add Text, Replace Background, and Reels12.

To explore Guided Edit Mode, adhere to the following steps:

1. Open the photo you wish to edit in the Photo Editor by selecting File > Open.

2. Transition to Guided mode by clicking on the Guided tab located at the top of the Photo Editor window.
3. Navigate through Guided Edits by category or utilize the search box to locate a specific one. Clicking the Explore button reveals hidden gems.
4. Select the desired Guided Edit and follow the step-by-step instructions presented on the right panel. Additional resources such as video tutorials or detailed technique explanations can be accessed by clicking links at the bottom of the panel.
5. Upon completing the Guided Edit, click Next to determine the next steps. Options include saving, sharing, or continuing the editing process in Quick or Expert mode.

Managing Photo Editor Preferences

Customizing Photo Editor Preferences allows you to put the application's settings and options to your specific needs and preferences. Accessing Photo Editor Preferences can be done by selecting Edit > Preferences or using the keyboard shortcut Ctrl+K (Windows) or Command+K (Mac). Type: Refine type settings, including font preview size, text engine, and smart quotes.

To modify preferences, utilize checkboxes, sliders, drop-down menus, or text fields within the dialog box. A search bar at the top-right corner facilitates finding specific preferences. Apply changes by clicking OK, and to restore default preferences, press and hold Alt+Ctrl+Shift (Windows) or Option+Command+Shift (Mac) when starting Photoshop Elements.

Examining the List of the Preferences Panels

The preferences panels in Photoshop Element 2024 provide a platform to tailor a variety of settings and options, including display, performance, file saving, cursors, and type, among others. To access these panels, navigate to Edit > Preferences (Windows) or Photoshop Elements > Preferences (Mac OS) in the menu bar. Alternatively, use the keyboard shortcut Ctrl+K (Windows) or Command+K (Mac OS) to open the Preferences dialog box.

Within the Preferences dialog box, a list of categories is presented on the left side, with each category housing its panel featuring distinct options. Users can click on a category to view the corresponding panel or utilize the search bar at the top right corner to pinpoint a specific preference. For instance, modifying the color mode of the app UI elements can be achieved by typing "color mode" in the search bar and selecting "Interface" from the results. This directs users to the Interface panel, where a neutral color mode can be chosen from the drop-down menu.

Several preference panels include:

1. **General:** Adjust fundamental settings like interface language, number of history states, default image interpolation method, and auto-update options.
2. **Display & Cursors:** Choose how images and cursors are displayed, covering zoom quality, screen mode, cursor size and shape, and the show crosshair option.
3. **Transparency & Gamut:** Set the appearance and color range of transparent areas, including grid size and color, gamut warning color, and transparency indicator.

4. **Units & Rulers:** Specify units of measurement and rulers for rulers, type, point/pica size, column size, and keyboard increments.
5. **Guides, Grid & Slices:** Customize guides, grids, and slices, such as guide and grid color and style, gridline and subdivision frequency, and slice options.
6. **Plug-Ins:** Manage plug-ins, including additional plug-ins folder, enable generator option, and enable remote connections option.
7. **Type:** Configure type settings, such as font preview size, use the smart quotes option, type unit, and Asian text options.
8. **File Handling:** Control file saving and opening, covering file compatibility, file extension, save in background option, and recent files list.
9. **Performance:** Optimize performance with settings like memory usage, scratch disks, history and cache options, and graphics processor settings.

CHAPTER SIX

MOVING AROUND THE ORGANIZER

Organizing your Hard Drive Photos and Media

The Elements Organizer offers a versatile platform for effortlessly navigating and organizing your expanding repository of photos and videos in diverse and personalized manners. It provides a range of functionalities that empower users to structure and manage their media collection according to their unique preferences and requirements.

One notable feature is the ability to create albums, allowing you to compile and categorize related photos and videos seamlessly. For instance, you could craft an album dedicated to the memorable moments captured during a summer trip to Europe, offering a cohesive and easily accessible collection of your travel memories.

Beyond albums, the Elements Organizer facilitates the sorting and management of your media based on various criteria, enhancing accessibility and utility. You can employ organizational categories such as people, places, events, and keywords to create meaningful associations and groupings within your media library. This dynamic approach enables you to swiftly locate specific content associated with particular individuals, locations, memorable occasions, or any customized keywords you designate.

This functionality not only streamlines your search and retrieval processes but also enhances the overall organization of your visual narrative. Whether you want to revisit family gatherings, relive vacations, or find specific images tied to particular themes, the

Elements Organizer provides a user-friendly interface for tailoring the organization of your media assets to align with the way you perceive and engage with your visual memories.

Familiarizing yourself with the Elements Organizer workspace is a crucial step to optimize your experience in managing and navigating your media collection. The workspace is thoughtfully designed with four distinct views: Media, People, Places, and Events. Each view serves a specific purpose, offering a nuanced approach to organizing and accessing your diverse range of photos and videos.

1. Media View

In this view, the focus is on the media content itself. It provides a comprehensive overview of your entire collection, allowing you to navigate through images and videos seamlessly. Media View serves as a central hub where you can explore your visual assets without any specific categorization, making it ideal for a holistic overview.

All of your imported pictures and videos are visible in the Media view. You can review and arrange them, change them with a single click, and carry out other actions.

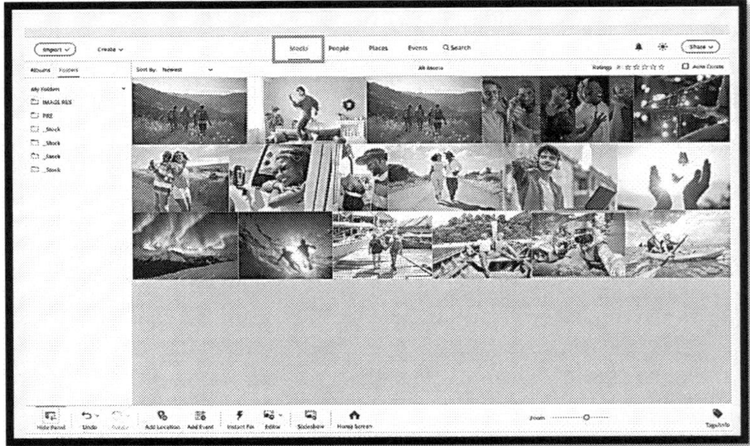

2. People View

People View is designed to streamline the organization of your media based on individuals featured in your photos and videos. This view employs facial recognition technology to automatically identify and categorize people, making it easier to locate content associated with specific individuals. It transforms your Elements Organizer into a personalized gallery, emphasizing the human element in your visual narrative.

The People view marks the faces of the people in your images so you can explore and arrange them more easily. Elements Organizer can build People stacks for you automatically when you import your images by spotting faces in the pictures that seem similar.

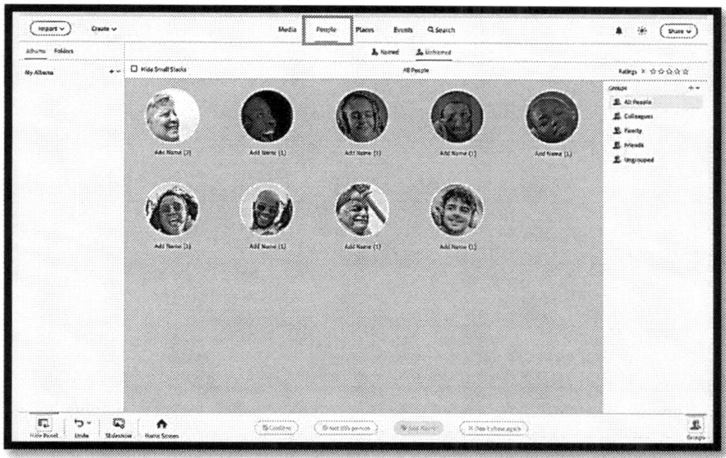

3. Places View

Places View provides a geospatial perspective, allowing you to organize your media based on the locations where they were captured. This feature leverages embedded location data, such as GPS coordinates, enabling you to revisit and explore visual memories tied to specific places. It's an excellent tool for reliving travel experiences or organizing content based on geographical significance.

Location data may be added to your images in the Places view. Because of this, it's simple to locate pictures from a trip you'd want to relive or a place you'd like to visit again.

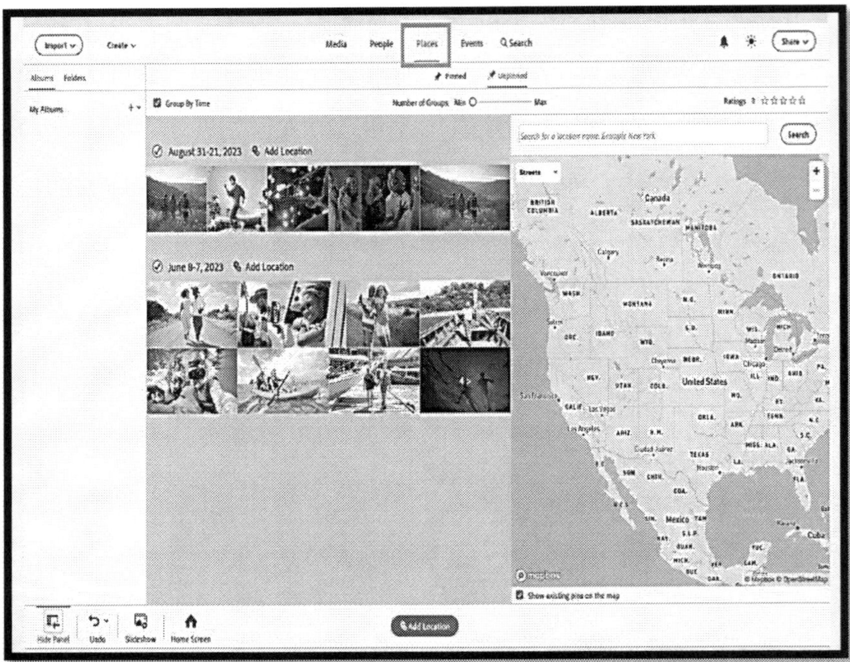

4. Events View

Events View focuses on the temporal dimension of your media collection. It categorizes photos and videos based on dates and occasions, making it convenient to revisit and organize content tied to specific events or timeframes. This view enhances the chronological organization of your visual narrative, aiding in the effortless retrieval of memories associated with particular moments.

Building picture stacks for various occasions is made easier using the occasions view. One possible use for this feature would be to create an event called Birthday Celebration and tag any pictures you want to link to it. That way, in the Events view, you can easily access all of the photographs that have the Birthday Celebration tag in one stack.

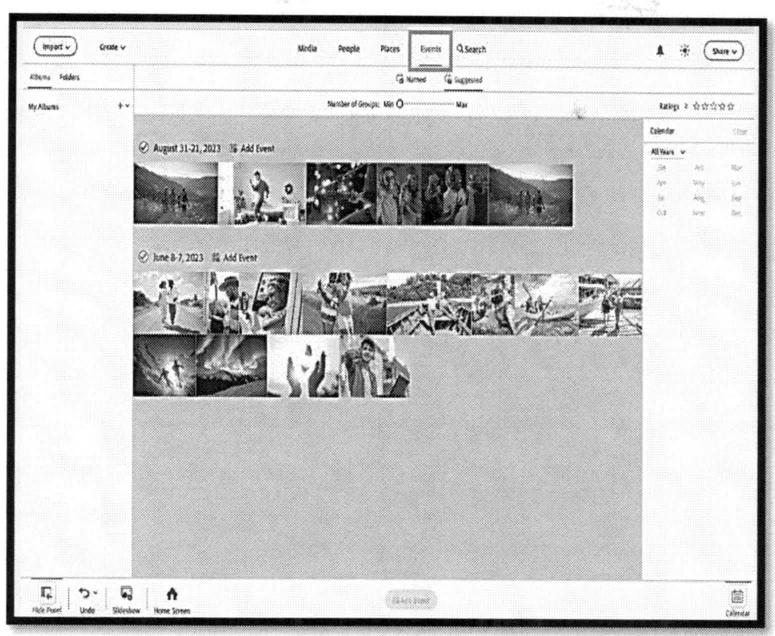

Adding Photos to the Organizer

Simplifying the process of importing media files, Elements Organizer provides a method to transfer content from your camera or card reader directly into its workspace.

Here's a step-by-step guide to seamlessly bring your media into Elements Organizer:

1. **Connect your Camera or Card Reader:**
   - Establish a connection between your camera or card reader and your computer.
2. **Navigate to Import:**
   - Within the Elements Organizer workspace, go to the Import menu.
   - Choose "From Camera or Card Reader."
3. **Configure Import Settings:**

- In the Photo Downloader dialog box, under Source, use the Get Photos From drop-down list to select the location from which you want to copy or import.
- Adjust the settings in the Import Settings area based on your preferences. You can either use default settings or customize them to suit your needs.

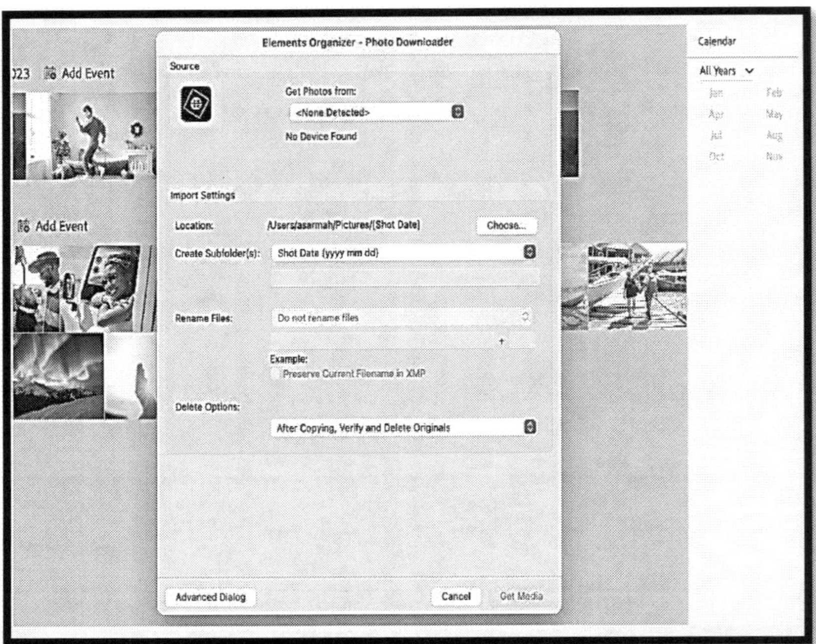

4. **Initiate Media Import:**
   - Click on "Get Media" to initiate the import process.
5. **Import Attached Keyword Tags (Optional):**
   - If the Import Attached Keyword Tags dialog box appears, select the keyword tags you wish to import.
   - Click "OK" to confirm your selections.
6. **Confirmation of Successful Import:**
   - After the import process is complete, a Files Successfully Copied dialog box will appear.

- Select "OK" to acknowledge the successful import of your media files.

Adding Files from hardware Folders and Removable Media

Efficiently managing your diverse collection of photos and videos becomes easy with Elements Organizer. You can import media from various sources such as your computer, CD/DVD, removable drives, or network locations. This allows you to curate and organize your visual content in personalized ways, from creating albums to tagging individuals within photos.

Elements Organizer offers versatile import capabilities, allowing you to import photos and videos from multiple sources, including your computer, CD/DVD, removable drives, or network places. You can also manage your media by creating albums to group related photos and tagging individuals in the photos.

When importing media from a folder on your computer's hard drive, Elements Organizer establishes a link to the media file within its catalog. The original file remains in its location on the hard drive unless you choose to copy or move it during the import process. Additionally, you can seamlessly import media files from external devices such as scanners, cameras, card readers, or phones. Elements Organizer follows a two-step process when importing from external devices, initially copying the media file into a designated folder on your hard disk and then creating a link to this copied file within the catalog.

Within Elements Organizer, starting the import process is easy and gives users a lot of control over their media. Here are the steps to follow:

1. Access Import Options

- Go to Elements Organizer and click on the Import tab.

2. Choose Source:

- Select "From Files and Folders" to import media from a specific file or folder location on your computer, external drives, pen drives, or network locations.
- Alternatively, you can also access this function through File > Get Photos and Videos > From Files and Folders.

3. Media Selection

- A dialog box will prompt you to choose the media you want to import. Navigate to the desired file or folder and select your media.

4. Optional Features

- Customize your import preferences by selecting optional features based on your needs, such as automatically fixing red eyes, suggesting photo stacks, copying import files, and generating previews.

5. Initiate Import

- Click "Get Media" to start the import process. This ensures that the selected media is brought into Elements Organizer according to your specified preferences.

6. Importing Keyword Tags

- Import keyword tags associated with your media by selecting the desired tags and clicking "OK." This helps maintain the organizational integrity of your media by importing and preserving applied keyword tags.

Import tags attached to media files

When handling media files equipped with keyword tags or metadata, Elements Organizer provides a comprehensive approach to importing and managing this valuable information. This ensures that the organizational integrity of your visual assets is preserved and seamlessly integrated into your catalog. Here's a detailed guide on how to import media files with keyword tags:

1. **Importing Media Files:**

   - Begin by importing your media files into Elements Organizer. For detailed instructions, refer to the documentation on importing photos and videos from folders.

Note: The Import Attached Keyword Tags dialog box will appear if your media files include tags or keyword metadata.

2. **Options in Import Attached Keyword Tags Dialog Box:**
   - Upon encountering the Import Attached Keyword Tags dialog box, choose from the following options:

a. **Select Tags to Import:**

- Choose specific tags to import, and they will be added to the Keyword Tags panel upon importing the media files.
- Tags marked with an asterisk (*) indicate that you already have a tag with the same name in your catalog. In such cases, the existing tag is attached to the media files.

b. **Advanced Options:**

- Click "Advanced" for additional customization options.

3. **Advanced Options:**
   - If you opt for the Advanced options, you can perform the following actions and then click "OK":

a. **Select Tags to Import:**

- Choose tags by clicking the boxes next to their names. Activating a tag enables options to the right of the tag.

b. **Rename Tags:**

- If you wish to rename a tag during import, select the tags, click the button next to "Import As New Keyword Tag Named," and enter a new name in the textbox. Elements Organizer adds a tag with the new name to your catalog and attaches it to the imported media files.

c. **Map Tags to Existing Tags:**

- To map an imported tag to an existing tag in your catalog, select the tags, click the button under "Use An Existing Keyword Tag," and choose a tag from the pop-up menu. The chosen tag name replaces the original tag name for the imported media files.

d. **Reset to Basic:**

- Click "Reset To Basic" to clear your changes and return to the Import Attached Keyword Tags dialog box.

Downloading your camera Image to the Organizer with Elements Downloader

In Photoshop Elements, you can use the Elements Downloader to import images from your camera to the Organizer. This feature allows you to easily organize and manage your photos.

To download your camera images to the Organizer using Elements Downloader, you can follow these general steps:

1. Connect your camera to your computer using a USB cable or insert the camera's memory card into your computer's card reader.

2. Open Photoshop Elements 2024 and go to the Organizer module.
3. Click on the "File" menu and select "Get Photos and Videos" or a similar option.
4. Choose "From Camera or Card Reader" or a similar option to launch the Elements Downloader.
5. Follow the on-screen prompts to select the images you want to import and specify the destination folder in the Organizer.

Establishing a seamless connection between your camera or card reader and your computer is the initial step in effortlessly transferring your photos. Navigate to the Organizer workspace, where a user-friendly process awaits you. Follow these steps to import your photos with ease:

1. **Hardware Connection:**
   - Connect your camera or card reader to your computer, ensuring a stable and secure connection.
2. **Access the Organizer Workspace:**
   - Open the Organizer workspace, providing a centralized hub for managing your visual assets.
3. **Initiate Import:**
   - Navigate to the Import menu and select "From Camera or Card Reader." This step kickstarts the import process, allowing you to seamlessly transfer your photos.
4. **Configure Source Settings:**
   - In the ensuing Photo Downloader dialog box, locate the "Source" section. Here, use the "Get Photos From" drop-down list to specify the source from which you wish to copy or import your photos. This versatile list includes options such as your camera, card reader, or other connected devices.

Managing the Media Browser

One essential part of the Organizer workspace is the Media Browser, which is a full-featured tool for organizing and engaging with your enormous picture and video library. These are some enlightening pointers to improve your knowledge and skills using the Media Browser.:

1. **Thumbnail Resizing:**
   - Customize your viewing experience by resizing thumbnails in the Media Browser. Simply drag the slider located at the bottom-right corner of the panel to achieve the desired thumbnail size, providing flexibility based on your visual preferences.
2. **View Mode Options:**
   - Tailor the presentation of your media by altering the view mode in the Media Browser. Click on the icons positioned at the top-right corner of the panel to toggle between Grid, Details, or Timeline views. Each mode offers a unique perspective, allowing you to choose the most suitable layout for your organizational needs.
3. **Filtering Options:**
   - Streamline your search for specific media files by employing the filter functionality. Click the "Filter By" button at the top-left corner of the panel to access a range of filter options. Filter criteria include date, keyword tags, albums, people, places, events, or smart tags, empowering you to pinpoint and organize your visual content with precision.
4. **Multi-Selection Techniques:**

- Expedite your media management tasks by mastering multi-selection techniques in the Media Browser. Select multiple media files effortlessly by holding down the Ctrl key (Windows) or the Command key (Mac) while clicking on thumbnails. Alternatively, choose a range of media files by holding down the Shift key and clicking on the first and last thumbnails in the desired range.

5. **Action Options:**

- Unlock the full potential of the selected media files by accessing a plethora of actions. Right-click on the chosen thumbnails to reveal a context menu, offering options such as adding files to an album, applying keyword tags, initiating edits in the Photo Editor, or facilitating online sharing. This nuanced approach enables a seamless workflow, allowing you to execute various tasks with ease.

Importing Photos with Scanner Plug-ins

Firstly, ensure that your scanner is properly connected and configured to interface with your computer. If necessary, download and install the latest scanner driver from the manufacturer's website.

Next, launch Photoshop Element and navigate to File > Import > WIA Support in the menu bar. This action initiates the Windows Image Acquisition (WIA) interface, enabling the direct importation of scanner images into Photoshop Element. Alternatively, use the keyboard shortcut Ctrl+Shift+W (Windows) or Command+Shift+W (Mac OS) to access the WIA interface.

Subsequently, choose your scanner from the device list and click next. A preview of the scan appears, allowing you to modify settings like resolution, color mode, brightness, and contrast via the Advanced Settings button. Additionally, you can crop or rotate the image by manipulating handles within the preview window.

Once satisfied with the preview, click next to commence the scanning process. The scanned image will be introduced into Photoshop Element as a new document, offering the flexibility to edit, save, or share the image according to your preferences.

Importing Phone Images to the organizer

Adding images and videos from your phone to Photoshop Elements Organizer is a simple procedure. Follow these comprehensive instructions after making sure your phone and computer are connected wirelessly or via a USB cord:

1. **Connect Your Phone:**
   - Establish a connection between your phone and computer using a USB cable or a wireless connection, ensuring a stable link for the data transfer.
2. **Access the Organizer Workspace:**
   - Open the Organizer workspace in Photoshop Elements 2024 to initiate the import process.
3. **Initiate Import:**
   - Navigate to the Import menu and select "From Camera or Card Reader" in the Organizer workspace. This step sets the stage for importing your photos and videos.
4. **Configure Import Settings:**
   - In the ensuing Photo Downloader dialog box, navigate to the "Source" section. Here, use the "Get Photos From" drop-down

list to specify where you want to copy or import from, selecting your connected phone.

5. **Customize Import Settings:**
   - Customize the import process by either using default settings or adjusting options in the Import Settings area based on your preferences.
6. **Get Media:**
   - Click on "Get Media" to commence the import process. Your photos and videos will be copied from your phone to your computer and seamlessly integrated into the Organizer.
7. **Manage Imported Media:**
   - Once imported, your photos and videos are ready for organization within the Organizer. You can now view, sort, tag, and edit them according to your preferences and creative needs.

Managing Organizer Preferences

Photoshop Elements Organizer can be effectively adjusted to your requirements by changing the options inside the program. Use these procedures to explore and modify these preferences:

1. **Access the Preferences Dialog Box:**
   - Open the Preferences dialog box by choosing either Edit > Preferences (Windows) or Photoshop Elements > Preferences (Mac) from the menu bar.
2. **Explore Categories of Preferences:**
   - Within the Preferences dialog box, explore various categories of preferences listed on the left side. These categories encompass a range of settings to customize your Organizer experience.

3. **General Preferences:**
    - In the "General" category, set options for the interface. Tailor aspects such as language, font size, color theme, and auto-hide panels according to your preferences.
4. **Media Analysis Preferences:**
    - Navigate to the "Media Analysis" category to enable or disable automatic analysis of your media files. This includes smart tags, people, places, events, and visual similarity, providing you control over the automated organization of your content.
5. **File Preferences:**
    - In the "Files" category, specify the location and naming conventions for imported, edited, and exported files managed by the Organizer. This customization ensures efficient file management aligned with your workflow.
6. **Backup/Synchronization Preferences:**
    - Configure backup and synchronization settings in the "Backup/Synchronization" category. Define preferences for catalog backup and restoration, along with synchronization options for media files with cloud storage.
7. **Sharing Preferences:**
    - Access the "Sharing" category to set preferences for sharing your media files online. Customize options such as image quality, privacy settings, and integration with social media accounts.

Using a Scanner

Utilizing a scanner in Photoshop Elements 2024 is a seamless process, provided you have a compatible scanner, the necessary driver installed, and a stable connection to your computer. Follow these steps to import photos from your scanner into either the Organizer or the Photo Editor:

Scanner Setup:

1. Ensure your scanner is compatible with both your computer and Photoshop Elements.
2. Install the scanner driver on your computer.
3. Connect the scanner to your computer, establishing a reliable connection.

Importing Photos from Scanner - Method 1 (Organizer):

1. Open the Organizer and choose File > Get Photos and Videos > From Scanner.
2. From the drop-down menu, select your connected scanner.
3. Choose the folder where you want to save your scans and define the desired file format.
4. Click OK, and you may encounter another dialog box to adjust scanner settings. Follow the instructions to complete the scanning and importing process.

Importing Photos from Scanner - Method 2 (Photo Editor):

1. Open the Photo Editor and choose File > Import > WIA Support.
2. Select your scanner from the list of devices and click OK.
3. In the WIA dialog box, preview the scan. Adjust scan area, resolution, brightness, and contrast as needed.
4. Click Scan to initiate the import process, bringing the scanned photo into the Photo Editor for further adjustments.

Additional Tips:

- For enhanced customization, explore the scanner settings in both methods to fine-tune scan parameters.
- Save your scans in a designated folder with an appropriate file format for easy retrieval.

Import Photos from a Scanner in Photoshop Elements

Importing photos directly from a scanner into the Organizer in Photoshop Elements offers a streamlined process, provided your scanner is appropriately connected and configured for compatibility with your computer. Follow these comprehensive steps for a seamless import experience:

Scanner Setup:

- Ensure your scanner is correctly connected to your computer and configured to function seamlessly.
- Download and install the latest scanner driver specific to your scanner model, ensuring optimal performance.

Importing Photos into Organizer:

- Open the Photoshop Elements Organizer window once your scanner is correctly set up.
- Navigate to the Menu Bar and choose "File > Get Photos and Videos > From Scanner..." Alternatively, click the "Import" drop-down button on the Shortcuts Bar, then select "From Scanner..." to open the "Get Photos from Scanner" dialog box.

Scanner Selection:

- In the "Get Photos from Scanner" dialog box, use the "Scanner" drop-down menu to select the connected scanner from which you wish to import the photo.

- If the drop-down displays "None Detected," double-check your scanner's connection and ensure it is powered on.

Destination and File Format:

- Confirm the default folder for saving scanned photos under the "Save Files In" label. To modify this location, click "Browse..." and select the desired folder in the "Browse for Folder" dialog box.
- Utilize the "Save As" drop-down to choose the preferred file format for saving the scanned image.

JPEG Quality Adjustment:

- If "jpeg" is the selected format, use the adjacent slider to adjust the image quality. Drag left to decrease quality or right to enhance it, providing flexibility in choosing the desired level.

It is essential to make sure your scanner is connected and set up correctly for your computer to import photographs from a scanner into Photoshop Elements Organizer. For best results, you may need to update your scanner driver.

Begin by opening the Photoshop Elements Organizer window. From the Menu Bar, navigate to "File," then choose "Get Photos and Videos," and finally, select "From Scanner..." Alternatively, you can access this feature by clicking the "Import" drop-down on the left end of the Shortcuts Bar and choosing "From Scanner..." from the drop-down menu.

In the "Get Photos from Scanner" dialog box, locate the "Scanner" drop-down to choose the specific scanner you want to import the photo. If the drop-down displays "None Detected," double-check that your scanner is connected and powered on.

Below the "Save Files In" label, you'll find the default folder where the scanned photos will be saved. If you wish to change this location, click the adjacent "Browse..." button to open a "Browse for Folder" dialog box. Navigate to the desired folder and select it, then click "OK" to set the new destination.

Utilize the "Save As" drop-down to choose the file format for saving the scanned image. If you opt for "jpeg," adjust the image quality using the adjacent slider. Move the slider left to decrease quality or right to increase it.

To initiate the scanning and importing process, click the "OK" button at the bottom of the "Get Photos from Scanner" dialog box. Depending on the installed scanner driver, you may encounter another scanner-dependent dialog box that allows you to specify additional scanner settings. Follow any instructions in these dialog boxes to complete the importation process successfully.

Understanding image requirements

Understanding the basics is necessary to work with Photoshop Elements and alter photos. The following are important things to remember:

1. **Image Size and Resolution:**
    - **Image Size:** This refers to the dimensions of the image in pixels. You can modify the image size in Photoshop Elements through the option Image > Resize > Image Size. Adjusting the dimensions directly impacts the quality and file size of the image.
    - **Resolution:** This denotes the number of pixels per inch (ppi) or dots per inch (dpi). It significantly influences image quality. You can fine-tune the resolution settings in Photoshop Elements to achieve the desired outcome.
2. **Image Mode and Color Depth:**
    - **Image Mode:** This dictates the number and type of colors an image can display. Common modes include RGB (red, green, and blue), CMYK (cyan, magenta, yellow, and black), and Grayscale. Photoshop Elements allows you to alter the image mode through Image > Mode. Choosing the appropriate mode is crucial for achieving the desired color representation.
    - **Color Depth:** This refers to the amount of data used to represent each pixel. Common depths include 8-bit (256 colors), 16-bit (65,536 colors), and 32-bit (16.7 million colors). Adjusting color depth is crucial for detailed and vibrant images.
3. **Image Format and Compression:**

- **Image Format:** This determines how image data is stored and displayed. Popular formats include JPEG, PNG, GIF, and PSD. The choice of format depends on the intended use and required features. Photoshop Elements provides flexibility in choosing the appropriate format through File > Save As.
- **Compression:** This influences how image data is reduced to save space. Compression methods can be either lossy or lossless. Lossy compression sacrifices some data to reduce file size, potentially affecting image quality. In contrast, lossless compression maintains image quality through advanced encoding algorithms. Tailoring compression settings ensures the balance between file size and image integrity.

Using scanner plug-ins (Windows)

Utilizing scanner plug-ins in Photoshop Elements 2024 on Windows involves ensuring compatibility between your scanner, computer, and software, along with the installation of the necessary scanner driver. The connection between the scanner and your computer is a vital step for seamless integration. Subsequently, you can effortlessly import photos directly from the scanner into either the organizer or the photo editor.

Here are two distinct methods for employing scanner plug-ins in Windows:

1. TWAIN Plug-In:

- The TWAIN plug-in serves as an interface that establishes a connection with compatible devices installed on your computer.

- Note that the TWAIN plug-in may not be consistently updated for new operating systems, potentially resulting in less reliable performance compared to alternative scanning solutions.
- To access the TWAIN plug-in, you must download and install the Adobe Optional Plug-Ins for Windows 2.
- Once installed, navigate to File > Import > TWAIN in the Photo Editor to initiate the scanning process.

2. **WIA Support:**

- The WIA (Windows Image Acquisition) support presents an alternative interface that facilitates the importation of images from your scanning device.
- This interface tends to be more compatible with newer operating systems and a broader range of devices.
- To activate WIA support, you need to enable the Additional Plug-Ins Folder in the Preferences dialog box within Photoshop Elements.
- Subsequently, access File > Import > WIA Support in the Photo Editor to seamlessly import images from the scanner.

Elements Organizer facilitates seamless connectivity with your scanner, enabling you to effortlessly obtain scanned images of your photos, negatives, and slides. The acquisition of images from scanners can be accomplished through two distinct methods:

1. **Scanner Driver Plug-in Module:** Utilize the dedicated scanner driver plug-in module packaged with your scanner. This software exhibits compatibility with the 32-bit Elements Organizer on Windows. Alternatively, it employs the TWAIN® interface to execute scans and subsequently opens the scanned images directly within the Elements Organizer.

Note: The TWAIN manager is exclusively supported on Windows.

2. **Standalone Scanning Software:** Leverage the standalone scanning software included with your scanner for the scanning process and saving of images. Subsequently, seamlessly integrate these scanned images into Elements Organizer through the following avenues:
    - Click on "Import" and opt for "From Scanner."
    - Navigate to "File," then select "Get Photos and Videos," and finally, choose "From Scanner.

Scanning on the Mac

Follow these steps to initiate the scanning process using Apple's Image Capture app:

1. Navigate to the "File" menu and select "Import." Then, choose "Images from Device."
2. The selected action will trigger the launch of Apple's Image Capture app.
3. In the left-hand column, peruse the list of DEVICES and choose the specific scanner you intend to use.

Note: If your scanner's name is absent from the list of DEVICES, ensure that the necessary software and drivers have been correctly installed, and verify the physical connection of the scanner.

4. Opt for "Create new Photoshop document" to seamlessly open the resulting scanned image in Photoshop, presenting it as a new document.
5. Set various options to customize your scanned image:
    - Specify color preferences.

- Adjust the resolution and size according to your requirements.
- Choose the destination folder for saving the scanned image.
- Assign a name and select the preferred file format.

6. Once your preferences are configured, click on the "Scan" button to commence the scanning process.
7. Upon completion, the scanned image will automatically open in Photoshop, ready for further editing and enhancement.

Scanning many photos at a time

Effortlessly enhance your workflow in Photoshop Elements by employing the Crop and Straighten Photos command to automatically duplicate, crop, and straighten individual photos within a scanned image. Follow these steps to achieve optimal results:

1. Begin by opening the scanned image within Photoshop Elements.
2. Navigate to the "File" menu and select "Automate." From the dropdown menu, choose the "Crop and Straighten Photos" option.

This powerful command streamlines the process of extracting individual photos from a scanned image while automatically adjusting and aligning them for a polished and organized presentation.

3. As you execute the command, Photoshop Elements will intelligently identify each distinct photo within the scanned image, creating duplicate copies while simultaneously cropping and straightening them. This automated process ensures that each photo is isolated and presented in its optimal form, ready for further editing or sharing.

Phoning in Your Images

It takes a variety of techniques catered to your devices to effectively move and edit your photos from your phone to your computer in Photoshop Elements, a flexible photo-editing program. Discover these popular methods for incorporating your smartphone photographs into your editing process with ease:

1. **USB Cable Connection:**
    - Connect your phone to your computer using a USB cable.
    - Open Photoshop Elements Organizer and select "File > Get Photos and Videos > From Camera or Card Reader."
    - From the list of devices, choose your connected phone, and follow the instructions to import your photos.
2. **Cloud Services Integration:**
    - Utilize popular cloud services such as iCloud, Google Photos, or Dropbox to sync your photos across devices.
    - Open Photoshop Elements Organizer and select "File > Get Photos and Videos > From Files and Folders."
    - Navigate to the folder where your chosen cloud service stores photos and select the images you wish to import.
3. Wireless Transfer Apps:
    - Employ wireless transfer apps like AirDrop, Send Anywhere, or SHAREit to send photos from your phone to your computer.
    - Open Photoshop Elements Organizer and choose "File > Get Photos and Videos > From Files and Folders."
    - Access the folder where your chosen wireless transfer app saves photos and select the desired images for import.

After successfully importing your photos into the Photoshop Elements Organizer using any of the aforementioned methods, seamlessly transition to the Photo Editor for comprehensive editing:

- Select the imported photos.
- Choose "File > Edit with Photoshop Elements Editor."
- Leverage the Guided, Quick, or Expert modes to apply diverse effects, adjustments, and enhancements to your images.

These versatile methods empower you to effortlessly bring your mobile photos into the Photoshop Elements editing environment, providing you with the flexibility to enhance and refine your images with ease.

Setting Organizer Preferences

Customizing the Elements Organizer to suit your specific requirements is made easy through the Organizer preferences. These preferences encompass a range of features, including the visual aspects, performance settings, backup configurations, and synchronization options for your media files. To tailor these preferences to your liking, follow these steps:

1. Open the Photoshop Elements Organizer window to gain access to the customization options.
2. Navigate to the preferences menu by selecting Edit > Preferences on Windows or Adobe Elements Organizer > Preferences on Mac OS.
3. From the list on the left, choose the specific preference category you wish to modify. These categories may include General, Media-Analysis, Backup/Synchronization, and more.
4. Fine-tune the settings within the selected category based on your individual needs and preferences. Should you require additional guidance on any particular option, click the Help button for detailed information.

5. Confirm and implement your changes by clicking the OK button. This will apply the adjusted preferences and close the dialog box.

If at any point you wish to revert to the default settings of the Elements Organizer preferences, you can do so by following these steps:

Hold down Shift+Ctrl+Alt on Windows or Shift+Command+Option on Mac OS.

While maintaining the key combination, launch the Elements Organizer.

This action will reset the preferences to their default values, providing a fresh starting point for your Elements Organizer configuration.

CHAPTER SEVEN

ORGANIZING YOUR PICTURES

Examining Organizer Window

The Organizer window serves as your central hub for seamlessly navigating, organizing, and managing your diverse array of media files, including photos and videos. Beyond basic file handling, it offers the functionality to craft albums, slideshows, and various creative projects directly from the Organizer window.

Breaking down the essential elements of the Organizer window:

1. **Menu bar:** This section houses a spectrum of commands and options integral to the Organizer's functionality, including File, Edit, Find, View, and Help. It serves as the command center for accessing diverse features.
2. **Shortcuts bar:** Positioned for quick access to common tasks and features, the Shortcuts bar is home to functions like Import, Share, Create, and Instant Fix, streamlining your workflow.
3. **Panel bin:** A repository for different panels presenting information and options for your media files, such as Tags, Info, Places, and People. It facilitates detailed management and organization.
4. **Media browser:** This interactive space displays thumbnails of your media files. It enables user-friendly operations like the selection, dragging, and dropping of media files, contributing to a seamless organizational experience.
5. **Tool options:** Customize to the tool selected in the Shortcuts bar (e.g., Import, Share, or Create), the Tool Options area displays and

allows modifications to specific tool settings, enhancing precision in your actions.

6. **Photo bin:** Offering a dynamic view of thumbnails for media files currently open in the Photo Editor, the Photo bin permits swift transitions between the Organizer and Photo Editor interfaces.

To enhance your user experience, the Organizer window's appearance and layout are customizable. The View menu provides options such as Grid, Details, Timeline, and Full Screen, allowing you to tailor the display to your preferences.

Moreover, the flexibility extends to the resizing and rearranging of different components within the Organizer window. By dragging borders or corners, you can resize elements like the Panel bin, enhancing visibility and efficiency. Similarly, the arrangement of components, such as relocating the Photo bin by dragging its tab to the left edge, caters to personalized workspace configurations. This adaptability empowers users to craft an Organizer window that aligns precisely with their workflow and organizational preferences.

TAGS

Tags serve as a fundamental organizational tool within the Organizer workspace, providing an effective means to categorize and locate your photos with ease. In this workspace, two distinct types of tags play pivotal roles: keyword tags and people tags.

Keyword tags function as descriptive labels that you can assign to your photos, offering a dynamic way to categorize them based on content, themes, or specific categories that are meaningful to you. For instance, you have the flexibility to create keyword tags for places, events, hobbies, or any other criteria that align with your organizational preferences. Additionally, the system supports the creation of hierarchical structures for keyword tags, enabling a more detailed and nuanced organization. For example, you could establish a hierarchy like Animals > Dogs > Labrador, allowing for a granular classification of your photos.

On the other hand, people tags are specifically designed for identifying and categorizing individuals featured in your photos. Leveraging the People Recognition feature, you can either automatically detect and tag faces in your photos or manually assign people tags based on your preference. Similar to keyword tags, a hierarchical structure can be implemented for people tags, offering a hierarchical breakdown of relationships such as Family > Smith > John.

To manage tags effectively, open the Tags/Info panel within the Organizer workspace. This panel becomes the command center for creating, editing, or deleting tags, providing users with a comprehensive overview of their tagging system. The versatility of tags is further enhanced through the ability to drag and drop tags directly onto photos, simplifying the organization process. Moreover, the Find menu serves as a powerful search tool, allowing you to effortlessly locate photos based on specific tags.

In summary, the dual functionality of keyword and people tags empowers users to create a structured and intuitive organizational system within the Organizer workspace. Whether through the descriptive power of keyword tags or the personal touch of people tags, organizing and finding your photos becomes a seamless and personalized experience.

Creating Photo Tag

Photo tags serve as descriptive keywords that facilitate the organization and retrieval of your images at a later time. These tags are particularly useful in managing and categorizing your photos efficiently. Creating and utilizing photo tags can be achieved through the following steps within the Photoshop Elements Organizer window:

1. **Creating a Photo Tag:** a. Open the Photoshop Elements Organizer window. b. Navigate to the Panel bin and click on the Tags tab to unveil the Tags panel. c. At the bottom of the Tags panel, click the new button and select New Keyword Tag from the ensuing menu. d. Input a distinctive name for your photo tag in the Name field. e. Optionally, choose a category, color, and icon for your photo tag from the drop-down menus. f. Confirm your selections by clicking OK, thus creating your photo tag.
2. **Assigning a Photo Tag:** a. In the Media browser, select the desired photo or photos for tagging. b. Drag and drop the photo tag from the Tags panel onto one of the selected photos. c. Alternatively, right-click the photo tag and opt for Apply Keyword Tag to Selected Items from the menu. d. For multiple tags, hold down the Ctrl (Windows) or Command (Mac OS) key while clicking on the photo tags in the Tags panel.
3. **Removing a Photo Tag from a Photo:** a. In the Media browser, select the photo or photos you wish to untag. b. Right-click on the photo tag to be removed and choose Remove Keyword Tag from Selected Items. c. Alternatively, click the photo tag in the Tags panel and press the Delete key.
4. **Deleting a Photo Tag:** a. Click on the specific photo tag within the Tags panel that you want to delete. b. At the bottom of the Tags panel, click the Delete button and select Delete Keyword Tag from the menu. c. Alternatively, right-click the photo tag and opt for Delete Keyword Tag from the menu. d. Confirm the deletion by clicking Yes when prompted

Changing Tag Icons

Tag icons are visual indicators that appear alongside your tags in the Tags panel of the Photoshop Elements Organizer window. These icons are important for quickly and easily identifying and distinguishing between different tags. Users can choose from a variety of pre-existing tag icons provided by Photoshop Elements, or they can create their personalized icons using images from their photo collection.

To modify a tag icon, follow these steps:

1. Open the Photoshop Elements Organizer Window:

- Launch the Photoshop Elements application and open the Organizer window.

2. Access the Tags Panel:

- Navigate to the Panel bin and click on the Tags tab to reveal the Tags panel.

3. Change a Tag Icon:

- Right-click on the specific tag that you want to modify the icon for.

- Select "Edit Keyword Tag" from the menu that appears.

4. Navigate the Edit Keyword Tag Dialog Box:
- In the Edit Keyword Tag dialog box, find the "Icon" drop-down menu.

5. Select an Icon:
- Choose an icon from the pre-existing options provided by Photoshop Elements.
- Alternatively, click the "Browse" button to select an icon stored on your computer.
- For a more personalized touch, click the "Create" button to generate an icon from a chosen photo.

6. Apply Changes:
- Confirm the alterations by clicking "OK" to apply the selected icon.
- The dialog box will close, and the updated icon will be associated with the respective tag.

7. Modify Multiple Tag Icons Simultaneously:
- For efficiency, select multiple tags within the Tags panel.
- Access the menu bar and choose "Edit > Edit Keyword Tags."
- Follow the same steps as outlined above to change the icons for the selected tags.
- Click "OK" to confirm the changes.

Sorting and Finding Photos via Tags

To efficiently organize and locate your photos based on tags, you can leverage both the Filter bar and the Search field within the Photoshop Elements Organizer window, providing a seamless and versatile experience.

1. Sorting Photos Using the Filter Bar:

- Navigate to the top of the Media Browser and locate the Filter bar.
- Click on the Tags icon to access tag-based filtering options.
- Select the specific tags you want to filter by, utilizing checkboxes to include or exclude subcategories of tags.
- This dynamic filtering process allows you to narrow down your photo selection based on chosen tags, streamlining your search and organization.

2. **Finding Photos Using the Search Field:**

- Utilize the Search field positioned at the top right corner of the Organizer window for a more targeted search approach.
- Type the name of the tag you wish to search for, and the Organizer will display matching photos in real-time.
- Explore advanced search capabilities by employing Boolean operators, including "and," "or," and "none."

3. **Combining Multiple Tags with Boolean Operators:**

- Employ Boolean operators to refine your search criteria and find photos with specific tag combinations.
- For instance, to locate photos with both the Keyword Tag "Vacation" and the People Tag "Jane," input "Vacation and Jane" in the Search field.
- For photos that have either the Keyword Tag "Vacation" or the People Tag "Jane," use "Vacation or Jane" in the Search field.
- To find photos with the Keyword Tag "Vacation" but without the People Tag "Jane," input "Vacation none Jane.

Adding Photos to an Album

An album serves as a curated compilation of photos within the Elements Organizer, offering users a means to systematically organize their visual content. The flexibility of albums allows users to aggregate photos from various sources, including their computer, camera, or card reader.

1. **Creating and Opening an Album:**
   - Launch the Photoshop Elements Organizer window.
   - Access the Albums panel by clicking on the Albums tab in the Panel bin.
   - If an album doesn't exist yet, create one by clicking the New button at the bottom of the Albums panel and selecting New Album. Input a name and category for the album and confirm by clicking OK.
2. **Adding Photos to an Album:**
   - Utilize multiple methods to add photos to your album:
   - Drag photos or videos from the Media browser into the album in the Albums panel.
   - Drag the album from the Albums panel onto photos in the Media browser.
   - Right-click the album in the Albums panel, select Add Selected Items to Album, and choose the desired photos or videos in the Media browser.
   - Right-click the photos or videos in the Media Browser, select Add to Selected Album, and choose the target album in the Albums panel.
3. **Adding Photos During Import:**

- Connect your camera or card reader to your computer.
- Access the Organizer workspace and select Import > From Camera or Card Reader.
- In the Photo Downloader dialog box, under Source, choose the location to import from using the Get Photos From drop-down list.
- Under Destination, select the album to which you want to add the imported photos from the Add to Album drop-down list. Create a new album if needed by clicking the New button next to the list.
- Choose the photos to import and complete the process by clicking Get Media.

These diverse methods provide users with flexibility in building and managing their albums seamlessly. Whether adding photos from existing collections or during the import process, Photoshop Elements offers an intuitive and customizable approach to organizing visual content. The creation and utilization of albums contribute significantly to an efficient and personalized photo management experience within the Elements Organizer.

Add photos to multiple albums

Click the "All Media" button in the upper-left corner of the Media view to begin accessing and organizing your material in the Organizer. By doing this, you can see every piece of material that is accessible inside the vast library of the Organizer.

Once within the Media view, streamline your selection process by choosing one or more photos. A distinctive blue outline will highlight the selected photos, providing a clear visual indicator of your chosen items.

For an organized approach, navigate to the Albums panel and select one or more album names. Employ the Shift-click method to select items consecutively or utilize the Ctrl-click (Windows) or Command-click (Mac OS) method for nonadjacent selections. This versatile selection mechanism allows you to pinpoint the albums that align with your organizational goals.

Now, seamlessly integrate your selected photos with the chosen albums using one of the following methods:

1. **Drag Photos into Albums:**
   - Directly drag the selected photos into any of the chosen albums featured in the Albums panel. This intuitive action swiftly associates the photos with the respective albums, facilitating a structured arrangement.
2. **Drag Albums onto Photos:**
   - Alternatively, enhance efficiency by dragging the selected albums from the Albums panel onto any of the chosen photos in the Media view. This reciprocal action achieves the same outcome, solidifying the connection between the selected albums and photos.

Editing Photo Album

Use these detailed instructions to easily improve and customize your photo albums:

1. **Launch Photoshop Elements and Access Organizer Workspace:** Begin by launching Photoshop Elements and navigating to the Organizer workspace, providing a centralized hub for managing your multimedia content.
2. **Select or Create an Album:** In the Albums panel, choose the album you wish to edit. Alternatively, create a new album by

clicking the + icon and selecting Album from the options presented.

3. **Add Photos to the Album:** Populate your album by dragging and dropping photos directly from the Media Browser or the Photo Bin. Alternatively, utilize the Add Media button to import photos from your computer or other sources.
4. **Remove Photos from the Album:** Streamline your album content by selecting unwanted photos and either pressing the Delete key or clicking the Remove from Album button.
5. **Rearrange Photo Order:** Tailor the visual narrative of your album by rearranging the order of photos. Drag and drop them to your desired positions, or utilize the Sort By menu to organize them by name, date, or rating.
6. **Edit Album Properties:** Fine-tune the album's attributes by clicking the Edit Album button. Adjust the name, description, or cover photo, and explore changing the album type from Standard to Instant Fix, Smart, or Video Story.
7. **Edit Photos Within the Album:** Dive into the individual photos within the album by selecting them and clicking the Editor button. This action opens the Photo Editor workspace, offering Quick, Guided, and Expert modes to apply a diverse range of edits and effects to your photos.
8. **Save Changes:** After refining your album and photo edits, click the Save button in the upper-right corner of the Photo Editor. Alternatively, employ the File menu to save, export, or print your photos according to your preferences.
9. **Share Your Album:** Extend the reach of your creative endeavors by clicking the Share button in the upper-right corner of the Organizer. Choose from various sharing options, including social

media platforms such as Facebook, Flickr, or SmugMug. Additionally, consider creating captivating slideshows, collages, or greeting cards to showcase your album dynamically.

Accessing, Deleting, and Renaming Photo Album

Albums in Photoshop Elements Organizer are digital representations of actual picture albums that let you arrange and store your photographs in a way that suits you. You may create, edit, rename, combine, and delete digital photo albums using Elements Organizer like organizing images in a physical album. Furthermore, the ability to exclude certain images from an album adds to the software's adaptable and user-friendly organizing features.

Editing an Album:

To refine the content and details of an album, follow these simple steps:

1. **Select an Album:** Navigate to the Albums panel within the Organize workspace and choose the specific album you wish to edit.

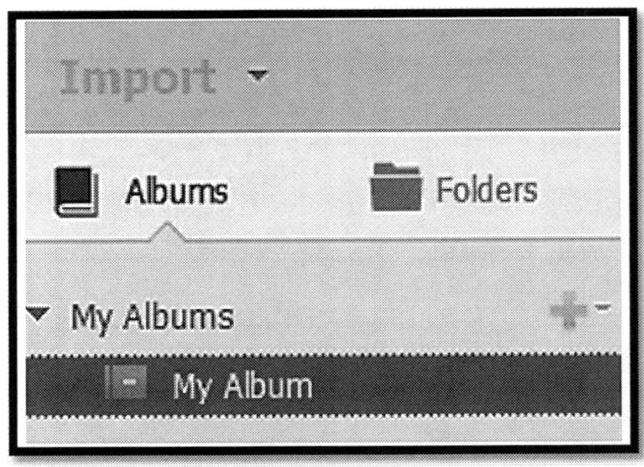

2. **Access Editing Options:** Depending on your operating system, employ one of the following methods:
    - Windows: Right-click on the chosen album and select "Edit."
    - Mac OS: Control+click on the album and choose "Edit."

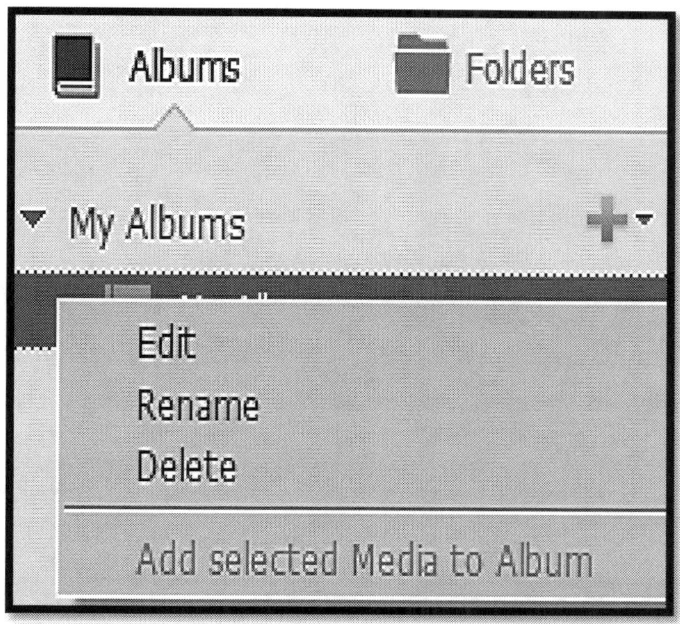

3. **Edit Album Panel:** Enter the Edit Album panel, where you gain control over various aspects of the album:

    - Name: Modify the name of the album to better reflect its content or purpose.
    - Category: Choose a category from the drop-down list, enhancing organizational clarity.
    - Media Deletion: Delete media effortlessly by selecting a photo or video and dragging it to the trash bin. The convenience extends to selecting multiple media items and dropping them into the trash bin as well.

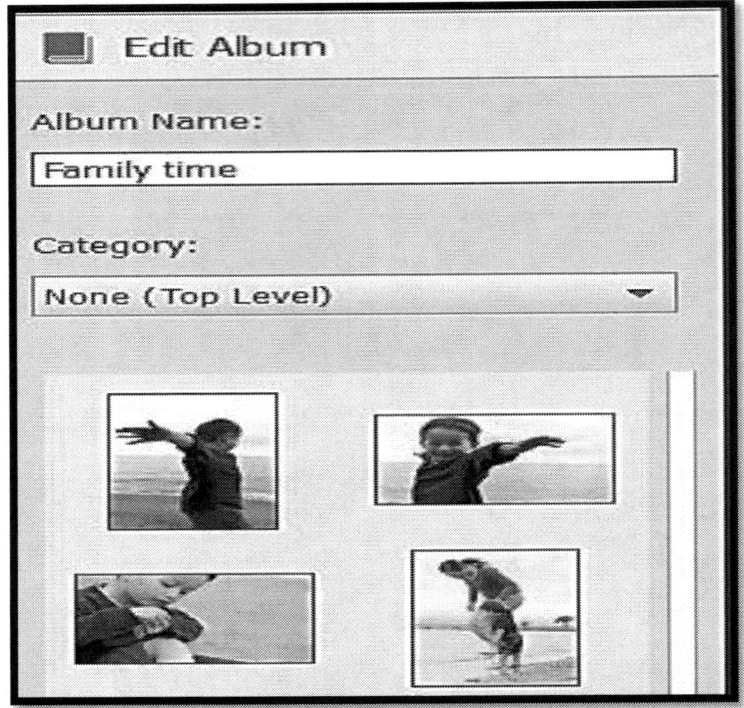

Rename an album

To rename an album in Photoshop Elements Organizer, follow these simple steps:

1. **Select the Album:** Choose the album you want to rename within the Organize workspace.
2. **Renaming on Windows:** If you are using Windows, right-click on the selected album. A context menu will appear, from which you can choose the "Rename" option.
3. **Renaming on Mac OS:** For Mac OS users, perform a Control+click on the album you wish to rename. This action will open a contextual menu where you can select the "Rename" option.
4. **Enter the New Name:** A Rename dialog box will appear after selecting the "Rename" option. In this dialog box, input the new desired name for the album.

5. **Confirm the Change:** After entering the new name, click the "OK" button to confirm and apply the changes.

Photoshop Elements Organizer allows you to manage your digital picture albums more effectively by allowing you to quickly delete photographs from individual albums without erasing them from the whole collection. To ensure a flawless removal procedure, adhere to the following instructions:

Removing Photos from an Album

1. **Select Photos in Media View:** Navigate to the media view and select the photos you intend to remove from a particular album.
2. **Choose Album for Deletion:** A photo can exist in multiple albums. Select the specific album from which you wish to delete the chosen photos.
3. **On Windows:**
    - Right-click on a selected photo.
    - Choose "Remove from Album" from the context menu.
    - Select the desired album name to complete the removal.
4. **On Mac OS:**
    - Control+click on a selected photo.
    - Choose "Remove from Album" from the context menu.
    - Select the specific album name to finalize the removal.

It's important to note that removing photos from an album does not erase them from the Element Organizer catalog.

Deleting Photos from the Catalog

If you wish to delete a photo from the entire catalog, follow these steps:

1. **On Windows:**
   - Right-click on the photo you want to delete.
   - Choose "Delete from Catalog" from the menu.
2. **On Mac OS:**
   - Control+click on the photo you want to delete.
   - Choose "Delete from Catalog" from the menu.

For additional confirmation before deleting from the hard disk, you can select the checkbox provided in the confirmation message.

By separating the process of removing photos from albums and deleting them from the catalog, Photoshop Elements Organizer ensures a safeguard against accidental data loss. This dual-step approach provides users with a more deliberate and controlled photo management system, allowing for flexible organization without permanent deletion.

Merge albums

Creating and updating albums is only the beginning of effective album management with Photoshop Elements Organizer; you can also combine numerous albums into a unified, well-curated collection. When combining related albums or fixing inadvertent duplications, this tool comes in extremely useful.

The Merging Process:

Consider a scenario where you've created both a "Cars" and an "Automobiles" album for the same set of photos. To streamline your organization, you can merge these albums into a singular, comprehensive "Vehicles" album, for instance. The resulting merged album encompasses all the photos from the original albums, eliminating redundancy and simplifying your photo library.

When you choose to merge albums, all photos are seamlessly integrated into one cohesive album, and the source albums are automatically removed. Notably, the order in which the photos appear in the merged album mirrors their arrangement in the Albums panel. Moreover, Photoshop Elements Organizer offers the flexibility to rearrange the photo order both before and after the merging process.

Executing Album Merging:

1. **Selecting Albums:** In the Albums panel, choose the albums you intend to merge. Employ the following selection methods:
   - Click on an album name to select a single album.
   - Shift-click for a contiguous selection of albums.
   - Control+click (Windows) or Command+click (Mac OS) for a noncontiguous selection.
2. **Initiating the Merge:** Depending on your operating system, execute the following:
   - **Windows:** Right-click on the selected albums and choose "Merge Albums."
   - **Mac OS:** Control+click on the chosen albums and select "Merge Albums."
3. **Selecting the Destination Album:** A prompt will appear with a list of available albums. Choose the destination album into which you want to merge the selected albums and click "OK."

By integrating this merging feature, Photoshop Elements Organizer provides users with a powerful tool for maintaining a streamlined and organized photo library. Whether merging duplicate albums or categorizing related content, this functionality ensures that your photo collections remain well-structured and clutter-free.

Reorganize albums and album categories

The top-level albums and album categories in Photoshop Elements Organizer are arranged alphabetically by default, providing a structured arrangement for simple access. But, if users would rather have a customized setup, the program provides an easy way to rearrange albums as well as the categories that go with them. Here's how to manage the organizational structure of your albums:

Enabling Manual Sorting:

1. **On Windows:**
   - Navigate to Edit > Preferences > Keyword Tags and Albums.
2. **On Mac OS:**
   - Go to Elements Organizer > Preferences > Keyword Tags and Albums.
3. **Enable Manual Sorting:**
   - Within the Preferences window, under the "Enable Manual Sorting Option," select "Manual" for both Album Categories and Albums.
   - Click "OK" to confirm the changes.

Reorganizing Albums and Categories:

1. **Access the Albums Panel:**
   - Open the Albums panel in Photoshop Elements Organizer.
2. **Select Items:**
   - Choose one or more albums and album categories that you wish to reposition in the hierarchy.
3. **Initiate Drag-and-Drop:**
   - Drag the selected items to their desired locations within the album hierarchy.

4. **Dynamic Album Category Adjustment:**

    - When moving an album category, note that the items it contains will seamlessly shift along with it, maintaining the cohesion of your organization.

Adding Photos to the Event

Events function similarly to other keyword tags within the framework of Photoshop Elements. When you create an event, it automatically becomes visible in the Tags panel under the dedicated section labeled "Events Tags." The seamless integration of events into the tagging system allows for efficient organization and retrieval of photos related to specific occasions.

Adding photos to your event is a simple process. You can effortlessly select desired photos from the grid and then drag them directly onto the Events tag in the Tags panel, or drag the Events tag onto the selected photos. This intuitive method ensures a quick and hassle-free association of images with the corresponding event.

For enhanced customization, the Events panel provides a range of editing options. By clicking on the Edit icon within the Events panel, you gain access to modify essential details such as the start and end dates, description, and media content associated with the event. This feature empowers users to curate a comprehensive and personalized representation of their events, tailoring the metadata to suit their preferences.

Furthermore, the versatility of events extends beyond photos, encompassing videos as well. Users have the flexibility to incorporate both photos and videos seamlessly into the event, allowing for a cohesive and multimedia-rich compilation of memories. This integration of different media types enhances the storytelling aspect of events, providing a more immersive and dynamic experience for users as they revisit and share their cherished moments.

Adding icons to tags

Icons serve as small, visually appealing images that allow you to personalize and enhance the aesthetics of your tags. In your tagging system, these icons can be chosen from a selection of default images provided by the software, or you have the option to import your images to use as icons.

To seamlessly integrate icons into your tags, follow these step-by-step instructions:

1. Open the Organizer and navigate to the Tags panel, located on the right side of the window.
2. Right-click on the specific tag to which you want to add an icon, and from the ensuing menu, select "Edit Keyword Tag Icon."
3. In the "Edit Keyword Tag Icon" dialog box that appears, you can peruse and select an icon from the default options by clicking on the desired image. Alternatively, if you prefer to use a custom image, click on the "Import" button.
4. If you choose to import a custom image, a new window will open. Navigate to the location where the image is stored, select it, and click on the "Open" button. This action will bring you back to the "Edit Keyword Tag Icon" dialog box.
5. Once you have chosen or imported your desired icon, click on the "OK" button to apply it to the selected tag.
6. Repeat these steps for any other tags you wish to customize with icons. Furthermore, you have the flexibility to modify or remove icons at a later time. To do so, right-click on the tag, select "Edit

Keyword Tag Icon" again, and follow the same process to make adjustments.

By incorporating icons into your tags, you not only enhance the visual appeal of your organization but also infuse a personal touch into your tagging system. This customization allows you to create a more visually engaging and meaningful representation of your digital content.

Working with custom tags

Custom tags in the Elements Organizer empower you to create and assign personalized labels to your photos and videos, enhancing the efficiency of your media organization. These tags come in various types, including keyword tags, people tags, place tags, and event tags, offering a versatile system for categorizing and locating your digital content.

To craft a custom tag, utilize the New drop-down menu within the Tags panel. Choose the type of tag you wish to create, whether it's a keyword, people, place, or event tag. Subsequently, assign a name to the tag, and effortlessly drag and drop it onto the photos or videos you intend to tag. This streamlined process ensures a quick and intuitive organization of your media.

For an added touch of personalization, you have the option to incorporate icons into your custom tags. This can be achieved by right-clicking on the tag, selecting "Edit Keyword Tag Icon" from the menu, and then choosing a default icon or importing your image. The inclusion of icons not only enhances the visual appeal of your tags but also contributes to a more engaging and meaningful representation of your digital library.

Should the need arise, you can modify or delete your custom tags at any time. A simple right-click on the tag allows you to access the appropriate options in the menu, facilitating easy adjustments to your organizational structure.

To refine your search and further streamline your media retrieval process, you can combine different types of custom tags. For instance, you might search for photos that feature both a people tag and a keyword tag using the search field in the Organizer. This ability to integrate and leverage multiple tag types enhances the granularity of your searches, making it easier to pinpoint specific media within your collection.

Working with default tags

Default tags within the Elements Organizer are automatically generated and assigned to your photos and videos based on metadata such as date, time, camera model, file type, and location. These tags are conveniently accessible in the Tags panel, and neatly categorized under the Default Tags section.

Utilizing default tags provides a valuable tool for filtering and locating your media within the organizer. This automated categorization streamlines the process of organizing and retrieving content based on inherent metadata attributes. As a user, you have the flexibility to navigate and explore your collection by leveraging these default tags to enhance your overall organizational efficiency.

While default tags offer useful categorization, they also provide a degree of customization. You can edit or delete default tags as needed, simply by right-clicking on them and selecting the appropriate option from the menu. However, it's important to note that the creation of new default tags or the addition of icons to existing default tags is not supported.

To further optimize your media organization, you can seamlessly combine default tags with custom tags you create, such as keyword tags, people tags, place tags, and event tags. This synergistic approach allows you to refine search results and implement a more nuanced organizational structure. For instance, you might perform a search for photos that possess both a date tag and a keyword tag using the search field in the Organizer. This capability enhances your ability to precisely locate and manage media content, offering a comprehensive and tailored approach to organizing your digital library.

Working with sub-categories

Sub-categories provide a valuable mechanism for establishing a structured hierarchy within the Organizer workspace for both keyword tags and people tags. This hierarchical organization proves especially beneficial when dealing with a diverse range of content, allowing for a more nuanced and granular classification of photos. For instance, you can create sub-categories like "Dogs" under the broader category "Animals," and further refine them by establishing sub-categories for different dog breeds, such as "Labrador," "Poodle," or "Beagle."

To create a sub-category efficiently, adhere to the following steps:

1. Open the Tags/Info panel and select the appropriate tab, either Keywords or People, based on the type of tag you wish to create a sub-category for.
2. Right-click on an existing category or sub-category within the panel and select "New Sub-Category" from the context menu.
3. Enter a suitable name for the sub-category and click OK to confirm.

4. Populate the sub-category by dragging and dropping relevant tags onto it. Alternatively, you can right-click on the sub-category and choose "New Keyword Tag" or "New Person Tag" to create new tags directly under the sub-category.
5. Efficiently manage your sub-categories by utilizing the context menu. Right-clicking on a sub-category provides options to edit, delete, or rename it as needed.

This systematic approach to sub-categories enhances the overall organization of your photos within the workspace. Whether you are dealing with keyword tags for content, themes, or categories, or people tags for faces in photos, the ability to establish a hierarchical structure significantly streamlines the process of managing and accessing your media content. By following these steps, users can ensure a more detailed and customized organization of their photos based on specific criteria and preferences.

Auto Generating Tags

Auto-Generating Tags is a standout feature introduced in Photoshop Element 2024, designed to streamline the organization and retrieval of your photos and videos based on their inherent content. Through the advanced functionality of Elements Organizer, this feature intelligently analyzes your media, automatically assigning pertinent tags, termed Smart Tag, which encapsulate various aspects such as Family, Children, Park, Beach, Smile, Ocean, Flowers, Sunset, Garden, and Soccer.

Leveraging Smart Tags, users gain the ability to efficiently filter and search through their expansive collection of photos and videos within the Organizer workspace. Furthermore, the integration of Smart Tags facilitates seamless editing, sharing, and album creation, offering a cohesive experience for managing multimedia content.

Should you find the need to refine or modify the Smart Tags associated with a particular photo or video, the process is easy. Simply right-click on the media element in question, and from the contextual menu, opt to Remove Smart Tag. This intuitive feature empowers users with the flexibility to tailor their media organization according to their preferences, ensuring a personalized and efficient workflow.

Working with Auto Creations

Auto Creations stand as personalized compilations, slideshows, and photo enhancements automatically generated by Elements based on the photos and videos you import. This feature adds a dynamic and creative dimension to your multimedia experience, allowing you to effortlessly view, edit, save, and share these bespoke creations directly from the Home screen or the Elements Organizer.

Accessing Auto Creations is a simple process. Launch either Photoshop Elements or Premiere Elements and navigate to the Home screen. Under the Auto Creations section, peruse the initial five creations using the numbered icons located below the thumbnails. For a comprehensive overview, click on View All to explore the entire roster of auto-generated elements within Elements.

For those seeking to customize an Auto Creation, simply click Open on the desired creation to access it within its respective Elements application. This grants you the freedom to make adjustments to the layout, style, music, text, and other elements of the creation, tailoring it to your artistic preferences.

To preserve your modified creation, click Save located in the upper-right corner of the Elements application. Here, you have the option to save the creation as a project file or export it as a video or image file, providing flexibility and versatility in managing your personalized content.

Sharing your Auto Creations is as simple as clicking on the Share button in the upper-right corner of the Elements application. This feature enables you to effortlessly share your creations across various social media platforms, including but not limited to Facebook, YouTube, Vimeo, and Twitter, ensuring that your uniquely crafted multimedia pieces reach a wider audience. The Auto Creations feature in Elements serves as an intuitive and enriching tool, enhancing the overall creative potential of your multimedia endeavors.

Rating Images with Stars

The inclusion of the star rating feature proves to be an invaluable asset, offering users a dynamic means to efficiently organize and filter their photo collections based on individual preferences. This feature allows users to assign star ratings ranging from 1 to 5 to any photograph within the Elements Organizer or the Photo Editor. The advantages of employing star ratings are multifaceted, contributing significantly to a seamless and personalized photo management experience.

One of the primary benefits of utilizing star ratings is the ability to expediently sort and view photos according to their assigned ratings. This can be accomplished effortlessly through the Sort By menu or the Filter panel in Organizer enabling users to quickly identify and access images based on their preferred rating criteria.

Furthermore, the functionality extends to the creation of smart albums, a powerful tool that automatically assembles photos meeting specific criteria, including star ratings, keywords, or dates. This automated album creation enhances efficiency in photo organization, ensuring that users can easily access and manage groups of images with shared attributes.

The star rating system proves particularly advantageous when it comes to selecting photos for various purposes, be it editing, sharing, or printing. Users can leverage star ratings as a quick reference to identify and work with the best-quality images in their collection, streamlining the editing and sharing processes.

Moreover, the compatibility of star ratings with other applications supporting metadata, such as Windows File Explorer or Adobe Bridge, adds another layer of versatility to this feature. The ability to sync star ratings across different platforms enhances the accessibility and consistency of photo organization, allowing users to seamlessly transition between applications.

To apply star ratings, users can follow the process. Simply select the desired photo in the organizer or photo editor, click the star icon below the photo thumbnail, and choose the appropriate number of stars. Alternatively, keyboard shortcuts (Ctrl+1 to Ctrl+5 on Windows or Command+1 to Command+5 on Mac) provide a quick and efficient means of assigning ratings. Should a user wish to remove a star rating, a simple click on the star icon and selection of "No Rating" accomplishes this, with corresponding keyboard shortcuts (Ctrl+0 on Windows or Command+0 on Mac) providing a swift alternative.

To ensure that the star ratings persist beyond the Elements Organizer, users can save the metadata to the photo file by choosing "File > Save Metadata to File." This ensures that the assigned ratings remain visible and accessible even when the photo is viewed in external applications, contributing to a seamless and consistent user experience.

Adding Images to an Album

Creating a personalized album in your photo management system is a straightforward process that enhances your ability to organize and showcase your cherished memories. Follow these step-by-step instructions to craft an album and seamlessly add images to it:

1. **Sort Your Photos:** Begin by navigating to the Media Browser and sorting through your collection to identify the photos you wish to include in your new album. This initial step allows you to curate a selection of images that align with the theme or narrative you have in mind for your album.
2. **Initiate the Album Creation:** Locate the plus (+) icon positioned next to "Albums" at the top of the left panel. Click on it to reveal a menu, and select "New Album" from the options provided. This action opens up the interface for crafting your customized album.
3. **Name and Categorize Your Album (Optional):** Take the opportunity to infuse personalization into your album by giving it a meaningful name. Additionally, you can select a category for your album to further streamline your photo organization. While naming is a crucial step, categorization is entirely optional and depends on your organizational preferences.
4. **Add Photos to Your Album**: There are two convenient methods to populate your album with chosen images. Firstly, drag and drop photos directly from the Media Browser into the designated "Content" tab within the New Album panel. Alternatively, select specific photos, right-click, and opt for "Add Selected Media."

These versatile options cater to your preferred workflow, providing flexibility in how you assemble your album content.

5. **Finalize and Save:** Once you've added the desired images, click on the "Done" button located at the bottom of the New Album panel. This finalizes the creation of your album and saves your selections. Your meticulously crafted album is now ready for viewing, sharing, or further customization.

Using albums for temporary work

Albums are a powerful feature in Photoshop Elements 2024 for arranging your picture library dynamically without requiring you to make any changes to the actual file locations on your computer. You may organize your images into projects, topics, events, or any other desired criterion using these flexible containers. Albums are especially useful for short-term assignments since they allow you to easily add, delete, or rearrange photographs, giving you a flexible way to manage your visual assets. Now let's look at some real-world examples of how to use albums for short-term projects:

1. **Creating a Dynamic Photo Collage or Slideshow:** Formulating an album tailored for a photo collage or slideshow begins by dragging chosen photos from the Media Browser to the Content tab in the New Album panel. Once assembled, delve into the Photo Editor to unleash your creativity—apply effects, adjustments, or text to enhance each photo. Upon completion, effortlessly export the curated album as a PDF, JPEG, or video file, showcasing your visual narrative with flair.
2. **Crafting a Personalized Photo Book or Calendar:** Tailor an album for a photo book or calendar by selecting a template from the Create panel. Populate the album with photos, then seamlessly

transfer them to the pages of the book or calendar. Personalization options abound as you fine-tune the layout, background, text, and embellishments. Once satisfied with the outcome, choose to order a printed copy directly from the Share panel or save your creation as a PDF file, preserving your visual story in a tangible or digital format.

3. **Efficient Photo Backup or Transfer:** For photo backup or transfer purposes, curate an album and select the desired photos from the Media Browser, transferring them to the Content tab in the New Album panel. Execute a backup or transfer seamlessly by utilizing the Backup/Restore command from the File menu or the Export As New Files command from the Edit menu. This enables you to safeguard your photos by saving them to an alternative location or onto a removable device, ensuring your visual memories remain secure and accessible.

Finding out more about sharing your albums

The possibilities available to you for sharing your carefully chosen albums are as varied as your artistic pursuits. Make use of these flexible channels to share your memories and visual tales:

1. **Digital Sharing Excellence:** Effortlessly share your albums with a global audience by exporting them as PDF, JPEG, or video files. With this approach, you can seamlessly send your creations via email, post them on social media platforms, or store them securely on cloud storage services. This digital sharing option ensures that your albums reach friends, family, or followers across the digital landscape, offering a convenient and instant means of communication.

2. **Tangible Keepsakes:** Elevate your sharing experience by ordering printed copies of your albums directly from the Share panel. This tangible option allows you to transform your digital creations into physical keepsakes, ideal for gifting or cherishing in your collection. Whether destined for your address or that of a friend, the Share panel facilitates a streamlined process to bring your visual narratives to life in a printed format.
3. **Seamless Cross-Device Accessibility:** Embrace the interconnected world of your creative endeavors by syncing your albums across devices using the Elements Mobile and Web companion apps (currently available in English-only beta). This feature extends the accessibility of your albums, allowing you to view, share, and manage them from any location. Whether you're on the go or at your desktop, the synchronization ensures a seamless transition between devices, fostering a cohesive and dynamic creative experience.

Adding People in the Media Browser

The Media Browser serves as a comprehensive panel within the Organizer workspace, showcasing all your photos and videos. It provides a versatile platform for efficient photo and video management. One notable feature is the People view, which facilitates the grouping of media based on the faces of individuals captured within them. This functionality greatly enhances the process of locating, tagging, and organizing your media content.

To incorporate individuals into the Media Browser, follow these step-by-step instructions:

1. Navigate to the People icon located at the bottom of the Media Browser within the Organizer.
2. Click on the + icon at the top of the People view and select the option to Add People.
3. In the ensuing Add People dialog box, meticulously choose the photos containing the faces of the individuals you wish to include. Employ the Filter By option to refine your selection based on date, album, keyword, or folder.
4. Click OK, prompting Photoshop Elements to scan the selected photos and autonomously identify the faces within them.
5. In the People view, the identified faces are presented in stacks, each stack representing an individual. Customize the arrangement by dragging and dropping stacks or merging them if they pertain to the same person.
6. To assign a name, double-click on the stack, input the name in the designated text box, and optionally add notes or relationships.
7. Confirm the name by clicking the checkmark icon or pressing Enter. Photoshop Elements will then automatically tag the photos in the stack with the individual's name.

Moreover, if Photoshop Elements fails to automatically detect a person, the Add Missing Person option can be employed through the following steps:

1. In the People view, click the + icon at the top and choose Add Missing Person.
2. In the Add Missing Person dialog box, select the photo containing the face of the person you wish to manually add.
3. Click OK, leading Photoshop Elements to open the photo in the Photo Editor.

4. Within the Photo Editor, utilize the Quick Selection tool to precisely outline the person's face, adjusting the tool size as needed with the bracket keys.
5. Click the Refine Edge button to fine-tune the selection, utilizing sliders and brush tools to enhance accuracy.
6. Confirm the selection by clicking OK, prompting Photoshop Elements to create a new stack for the person in the People view.
7. Follow the same steps as previously outlined to assign a name, completing the manual addition process successfully.

Placing Pictures on Maps

The Map-placing function is a potent tool that enables users to effectively organize and display their photo collection according to geographic regions. Located inside the Organizer workspace, the Places view is your starting point for exploring your images on an interactive map. You can easily add or edit location information and even create albums that are focused on certain locations.

Follow these procedures to place images on maps:

1. Launch the Organizer and click on the Places icon situated at the bottom of the Media Browser.
2. If your photos already possess location data, they will manifest on the map as pins. Use the zoom function, drag the map, or employ the search box to pinpoint a particular location of interest.
3. For photos lacking location data, rectify this by either adding it manually or automatically. For manual addition, select the photos and drag them onto the map. A dialog box will emerge, allowing you to input the place's name or select from a list of suggestions. Alternatively, for automatic addition, select the photos and click the

Add Location icon at the top of the Places view. Photoshop Elements will leverage the date and time of the photos to propose potential locations. Review and confirm the suggestions or make necessary edits.

4. To modify the location data of a photo, choose the photo and click the Edit Location icon at the top of the Places view. This provides the flexibility to alter the place's name, reposition the pin on the map, or entirely remove the location data.
5. Crafting albums based on specific places is a seamless process. Select the photos associated with the same location, then click the + icon at the bottom of the Albums panel. Opt for creating a New Album, input a suitable name, and witness the album materialize in the Albums panel, housing the selected photos within it.

CHAPTER EIGHT

VIEWING AND FINDING YOUR PHOTOS IN A CATALOG

Creating a Brand – New Catalog

When you import media files into Photoshop Elements, they are automatically included in the default catalog. If you decide to utilize this default catalog for all your media management needs, there's no additional action required.

Nevertheless, there are instances where creating multiple catalogs becomes advantageous. For instance, you might want to organize distinct catalogs for photos related to your workplace and those associated with your family.

To facilitate this, follow either of the procedures below:

- Navigate to File > Manage Catalogs.
- Use the keyboard shortcut Ctrl+Shift+C (Windows) or Command+Shift+C (Mac OS).

Upon accessing the Catalog Manager, if you're operating on a Windows OS, the following options will be presented:

- Choose "Catalogs Accessible By All Users" (Windows only) or "Catalogs Accessible By The Current User" to designate a preset location for the catalog.

Note: The Catalog Accessible by All Users and Catalog Accessible by the Current User options are unavailable in the Windows Application Store version of Photoshop Elements. The Windows Application Store version only provides two options: Default Catalog Location and Custom Location.

If you prefer a custom location, opt for "Custom Location," and then click "Browse" to pinpoint the location on your computer where you want to store the catalog file. Afterward, click "New."
Subsequently, in the "Enter a Name for the New Catalog" dialog box, input a name for the catalog and click "OK." This process ensures the creation of a customized catalog for your specific needs.

Importing Files to the New Catalog

The process of importing files into the new catalog is a method that empowers you to integrate your photos and videos into the Elements Organizer workspace without interruption. This versatile functionality allows you to draw files from a myriad of sources, including your computer, camera, scanner, mobile device, or even cloud storage. Here's an elaboration of the fundamental steps involved in importing files to the new catalog:

1. **Launch Photoshop Elements and Access Organizer:**
   - Open Photoshop Elements and navigate to the home screen.
   - Opt for Organizer to initiate the media management workspace.
2. **Manage Catalogs:**
   - Go to File > Manage Catalogs to access the Catalog Manager.
   - Select the newly created catalog from the list and confirm your choice by clicking OK. This action opens the chosen catalog in Elements Organizer.
3. **Get Photos and Videos:**
   - Continue by going to File > Get Photos and Videos within Elements Organizer.

- Choose the source of your files, such as Files and Folders, a Camera or Card Reader, a Scanner, or Mobile Albums.

4. **Follow On-Screen Instructions:**
   - Adhere to the on-screen instructions to specify the files you wish to import.
   - Configure import options according to your preferences, including choices like renaming files, stacking, or adding descriptive tags for efficient organization.
5. **Execute Import:**
   - Click the Import button to initiate the process, seamlessly incorporating the selected files into the new catalog.
6. **Alternative Method - Drag and Drop:**
   - Alternatively, employ a user-friendly method by dragging and dropping files directly from your computer into the Media Browser within Elements Organizer.
   - This drag-and-drop functionality streamlines the import process, making it even more intuitive and efficient.

Open a catalog

These simple procedures may be used to access and open a catalog in Photoshop Elements:

1. **Navigate to Catalog Management:**
   - Select the "File" menu, then choose "Manage Catalogs."
   - Use the keyboard shortcut Ctrl+Shift+C on Windows or Command+Shift+C on Mac OS.
2. **Access Catalog Manager:**
   - In the Catalog Manager dialog box, which opens as a result of the above steps, you'll find a list of available catalogs.

3. **Select Your Desired Catalog:**
    - From the list within the Catalog Manager dialog box, choose the specific catalog you wish to open.
4. **Initiate Opening:**
    - Click on the "Open" button to proceed.

Managing the Catalogs

The following actions may be taken to start Photoshop Elements' catalog conversion process: Click the "File" menu and choose "Manage Catalogs." Click the "Convert" button in the Catalog Manager. If your catalogs are kept in the default place, this operation will cause a new dialog to appear and provide a list of all of your current catalogs.

If, for any reason, your desired catalogs are not visible in the initial list, you can easily rectify this by clicking on the "Find More Catalogs" button. This prompts an option that allows you to navigate to the specific folder location where your catalogs are stored.

Upon clicking "Find More Catalogs," you'll be presented with an opportunity to explore and select the folder containing the catalogs you wish to convert. This flexibility is particularly beneficial if your catalogs are stored in non-default locations or on external drives. Navigate through your file system to pinpoint the appropriate folder, and upon selection, the catalogs within that folder will be made available for conversion.

This thoughtful design ensures that users have full control over the catalog conversion process, allowing them to seamlessly integrate and manage catalogs stored in various locations. Whether your catalogs are in the default location or spread across different folders, Photoshop Elements provides a user-friendly solution to streamline the conversion process and enhance catalog accessibility.

Create a backup for your Catalog

Establishing a backup for your catalog is a fundamental and prudent measure to safeguard your valuable data and organizational framework in the event of system crashes, upgrades, or transitioning to a new computer. This process enables you to preserve your catalog structure alone or include all your photos and videos. Moreover, you have the flexibility to opt for a comprehensive backup or an incremental backup based on your specific needs. To initiate the catalog backup process, follow these essential steps:

1. Navigate to the 'File' menu and select 'Manage Catalogs.'
2. Within the Catalog Manager dialog box, click on 'New.'
3. Provide a distinctive name for the new catalog and designate a location for its storage.
4. Confirm your selections by clicking 'OK.'
5. Proceed to the 'File' menu once again, this time selecting 'Backup Catalog.'
6. Choose from the available backup options: 'Backup Catalog Structure,' 'Full Backup,' or 'Incremental Backup.'
7. Specify the destination for your backup, whether it be a USB drive, hard drive, or network drive.
8. Complete the process by clicking 'Done' and patiently wait for the backup operation to conclude.

Restoring catalog Files

Restoring catalog files involves the retrieval of photos, albums, tags, and additional information from a previously created backup copy of your catalog. A catalog, essentially a database, holds essential data on your media files. Various factors such as power outages, disk failures, virus attacks, or software crashes may lead to catalog corruption or damage. In such instances, the restoration process allows you to recover your catalog, ensuring the seamless continuation of your work with photos and videos.

The procedure for restoring catalog files may vary based on the method of backup creation and storage location. Below are comprehensive steps to guide you through the process:

1. Launch Elements Organizer and navigate to File > Manage Catalogs.
2. Within the Catalog Manager, locate and click on the "Restore" option.
3. Browse to the specific location where you stored the backup of your catalog. This could be an external drive, a network drive, or a cloud storage service.
4. Select the backup file you wish to restore.
5. Choose the destination where you want to restore the catalog and its associated media files. You can opt for the default location or specify a custom one.
6. Initiate the restoration process by clicking on the "Restore" button. The duration of this process depends on the size of your catalog and the speed of your computer and drive.
7. Once the restoration is complete, click "Done." Subsequently, the restored catalog opens in Elements Organizer, allowing you to seamlessly resume your creative projects.

Switching to a Different Organizer View

Switching to a different organizer view is a way of changing how your media files are displayed and arranged in the Elements Organizer workspace. You can choose from different views, such as grid, timeline, map, people, places, events, and keywords. Each view has its advantages and features, depending on what you want to do with your photos and videos. To switch to a different organizer view, you can use the following steps: Open Elements Organizer and select the media files that you want to view. On the left side of the workspace, click the View menu icon (three horizontal lines). From the drop-down menu, select the view that you want to switch to. For example, if you want to see your media files in chronological order, select Timeline. If you want to see your media files based on their location, select Map. If you want to see your media files based on the faces that are detected in them, select People. The selected view will be applied to your media files. You can use the toolbar at the bottom of the workspace to adjust the zoom level, filter the media files, or change the sorting order.

Searching for Photos with the Search Panel

Exploring and retrieving specific media files is streamlined through the search panel, providing a dynamic means of locating content based on diverse criteria such as keywords, tags, ratings, dates, locations, people, events, and more. This robust functionality serves as a valuable tool for swiftly pinpointing and organizing photos and videos within the expansive Elements Organizer workspace.

Follow these steps to effectively utilize the search panel:

1. Open Elements Organizer and designate the media files you intend to search.
2. On the right side of the workspace, locate and click the search icon (🔍) to unveil the search panel.
3. Within the search panel, you can input a search term into the search box or leverage the available filters beneath to refine your results.

These filters encompass a spectrum of criteria, allowing for precision in your search. Additionally, the capability to combine multiple filters empowers you to tailor your search comprehensively.

4. Witness the search results materialize in the media browser, presenting the files that match your specified criteria. The toolbar at the workspace's bottom provides further functionality, enabling you to alter the view, sort the results, or apply additional filters for enhanced organization.

Viewing Photos in Memories (Slideshow)

Viewing photos in memory (slideshow) is a way of creating and playing a slideshow of your media files in the Elements Organizer workspace. You can choose from different themes, transitions, music, and captions to customize your slideshow. You can also save, export, or share your slideshow with others.

To create and view a slideshow, you can follow these steps:

1. **Selecting Files:**
    - Navigate to the Media view and choose the specific files intended for inclusion in the slideshow.
2. **Initiating Slideshow Creation:**
    - Under the 'Create' menu, opt for 'Slideshow.'
3. **Choosing a Theme:**
    - In the ensuing Slideshow dialog, select a theme that aligns with the desired aesthetic, such as a "memory" or an "array."
4. **Proceeding to Configuration:**
    - Click 'Next' to advance to the Slideshow Editor, where an array of settings awaits adjustment. Here, users can fine-

tune aspects like duration, transitions, music selection, and the inclusion of captions. The arrangement of media files within the slideshow can also be easily modified by adding, deleting, or rearranging them.

5. **Previewing the Slideshow:**
    - Click on 'Preview' to gain a glimpse of how the slideshow will appear with the chosen settings.
6. **Saving and Exporting:**
    - After perfecting the slideshow, users can click 'Save' to preserve it as a project file. Alternatively, choosing 'Export' allows the creation of a video file for broader sharing options.
7. **Playing the Slideshow:**
    - To relish the slideshow experience, opt for 'View' > 'Full Screen' or press F11. Convenient controls positioned at the bottom of the screen empower users to pause, resume, or exit the slideshow seamlessly.

Using Search

Searching for untagged items

Searching untagged objects is a handy way to find media assets that don't have keyword tags, smart tags, people, locations, or event relationships. When it comes to recognizing and categorizing images and videos that need more detailed descriptions, this tool is crucial.

To initiate a search for untagged items, follow these steps:

1. Open Elements Organizer and designate the media files you intend to search through.

2. Navigate to the right side of the workspace and click on the Search icon (🔍) to unveil the search panel.
3. Within the search panel, locate the filter icon (⚙) positioned beside the search box and choose "Untagged Items" from the ensuing drop-down menu.
4. The search results will promptly display all untagged media files in your catalog. To streamline your organization process, you can handpick the specific files you wish to tag and effortlessly relocate them to the corresponding tag within the Tags panel. Additionally, the creation of new tags is facilitated by selecting the 'New' button within the Tags panel.
5. Should you desire to eliminate the untagged items search parameters, simply click the 'X' icon situated within the search box.

Searching captions and notes

Explore and enhance your search capabilities within Elements Organizer by utilizing the Find By Caption or Note and Find By Details (Metadata) options. These functionalities empower you to locate specific captions or notes efficiently.

To initiate a search based on captions or notes, navigate to Elements Organizer and select Find > By Caption or Note. This action opens the Find By Caption or Note dialog box, providing you with a streamlined interface for your search.

Within the dialog box, enter a word or phrase in the designated textbox. If you wish to combine your caption or note search with additional criteria, opt for the Find By Details (Metadata) option.

For precision in your search, you can choose between two matching options:

1. **Match Only The Beginning Of Words In Captions And Notes:** This option targets media files and other items featuring notes or captions that commence with the same letters as your entered word or phrase. It ensures that your search results specifically include those files where the initial characters align with your input.
2. **Match Any Part Of Any Word In Captions And Notes**: Selecting this alternative broadens your search scope. It identifies photos and other files with notes or captions containing any fragment of the words you input. This inclusive approach ensures that even if your search term appears anywhere within a word in the captions or notes, the corresponding files will be included in the results.

Upon making your selection, click OK to execute the search, and Elements Organizer will efficiently retrieve the relevant media files based on your specified criteria. This robust search functionality enhances your overall experience by allowing you to tailor your searches to your specific needs, ensuring a seamless and effective organization of your media assets.

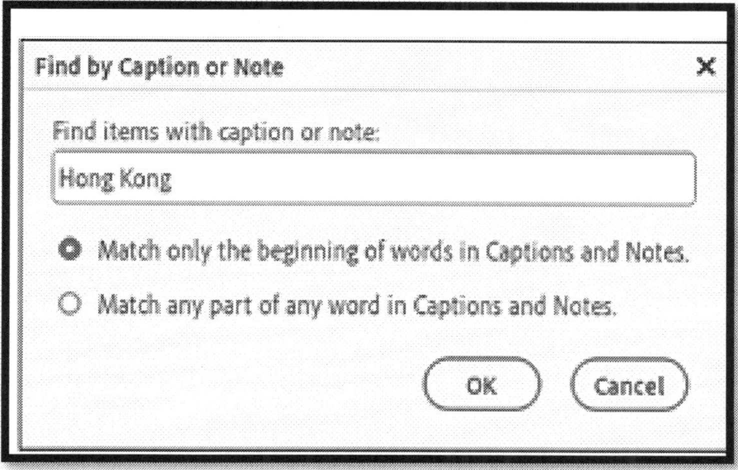

Searching by history

Elements Organizer provides a comprehensive solution for tracking the origins, usage, and sharing/export details of your media files. This functionality enables you to leverage a stored history, facilitating the efficient retrieval of photos and media files based on their usage and distribution.

To harness this capability, navigate to Find > By History in Elements Organizer. Within the By History submenu, a range of criteria commands await your exploration, allowing you to tailor your search based on specific parameters associated with the history of your media files.

Please note that certain options such as Exported On and Printed On are not accessible on Mac OS.

Upon selecting Find > By History, you'll be prompted to the "Select One Or More Groups You [Imported, E-mailed, etc.]" dialog box. Here, you can choose one or more items from the list that corresponds to your specified criteria. Clicking OK initiates the search process, enabling Elements Organizer to sift through the stored history and present you with media files matching your selected criteria.

It's essential to be aware that if you wish to permanently remove a particular history reference from the list, you can do so by selecting the respective item in the "Select One Or More Groups You [Imported, E-mailed, etc.]" dialog box. Subsequently, click the Delete button or press Delete on your keyboard. However, please note that the Delete button is not available for searches based on Imported On or Used In Projects histories.

This feature not only streamlines your media organization but also empowers you to manage the historical aspects of your files efficiently. Whether you need to trace the source of a media file, understand its usage, or ascertain its distribution, Elements Organizer's By History function offers a robust and user-friendly tool for these purposes.

Searching metadata

Use Elements Organizer's robust Find By Details (Metadata) feature to realize the full potential of your picture collection. This tool offers a sophisticated method for arranging and finding your media assets by enabling you to do extensive searches based on different file attributes and information related to your photographs.

When you have specific criteria in mind and wish to conduct a targeted search using multiple parameters simultaneously, the Find By Details (Metadata) dialog box becomes an invaluable tool. For instance, imagine you want to locate all photos captured on 12/01/2024 that are tagged with "Mom." In such cases, this dialog box allows you to seamlessly search for both capture date and keyword tags, streamlining your search process.

The searchable metadata encompasses a broad range of criteria, providing a versatile set of options for refining your search. These criteria include information about people, places, events, filenames, file types, tags, albums, notes, authors, capture dates, camera models, shutter speeds, and F-stops. It's noteworthy that when searching for camera raw files, Elements Organizer also includes TIFF files with a .tif extension in the results.

To initiate a search using the Find By Details (Metadata) dialog box, follow these steps:

1. In the Elements Organizer, navigate to Find > By Details (Metadata).

2. In the dialog box, select a metadata type from the first pop-up menu.
3. Choose a range for the search in the second pop-up menu, such as Starts With, Is Greater Than, or Contains. This instructs Elements Organizer on how to use the text entered in the third pop-up menu. Note that not all criteria include a second pop-up menu.
4. In the third pop-up menu, type or select the metadata name or value you want to find.
5. To include additional metadata values in your search, click the plus (+) sign, and specify values for the two or three pop-up menus that appear.
6. To remove metadata from your search, click the minus (-) sign next to the third pop-up menu for the metadata you wish to exclude.
7. Optionally, enable "Save this search criteria as a saved search" and enter a name for the search.
8. Click "Search" to execute the search based on your specified metadata criteria.

Additionally, if you want to modify your search criteria, you can do so by clicking on Options > Modify Search Criteria in the Find bar, making the desired changes, and then clicking Search. This feature ensures flexibility and adaptability in refining your searches as needed.

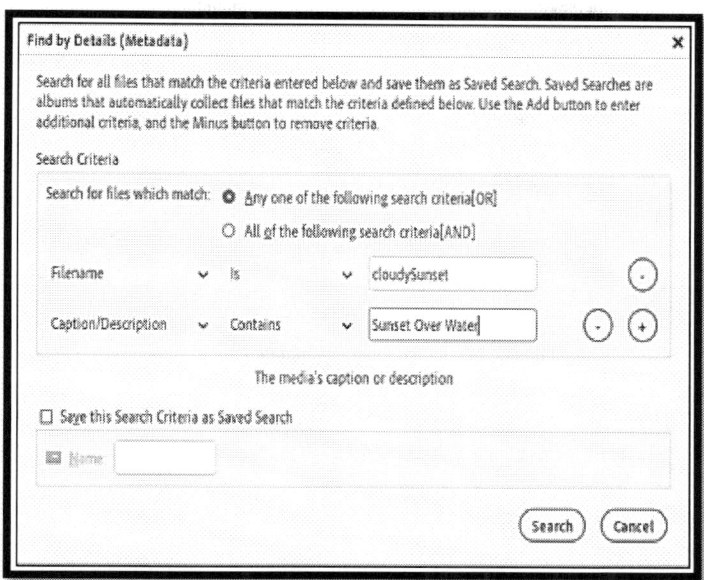

Searching similarities

Discover a range of sophisticated search options in Elements Organizer that are intended to improve your picture management workflow. Using a dynamic method, the Visual Similarity Search function finds photographs with similar items, colors, or forms. Discover how to use this tool to find visually similar material in your picture collection with ease. Use the color-shape slider to fine-tune your search criteria, allowing you to indicate the relative importance of colors and forms in your search for visually comparable photos.

For a more targeted exploration, the Object Search feature stands as an invaluable option. This functionality empowers you to handpick an object within a photo and initiate a search for other photos containing identical or similar objects. For instance, you can pinpoint your beloved pet dog in one photo and swiftly locate additional images that feature your cherished canine companion. This precise and intuitive feature streamlines the process of assembling a collection of photos centered on specific objects of interest.

Taking efficiency a step further, the Duplicate Photo Search feature proves indispensable for managing your photo collection. This feature excels in identifying and organizing photos that are identical or closely similar, including those captured in multi-burst mode. Once identified, you have the flexibility to arrange these photos as you see fit—stack, unstack, expand, or collapse them according to your preferences. This functionality not only declutters your library but also facilitates a more organized and streamlined viewing experience.

Make use of these search options' adaptability to improve your workflow for managing photos. Elements Organizer offers a range of features that address your various demands, whether you are looking for visually similar photographs, need to identify certain items, or need to effectively handle duplicates. These tools not only help you save time but also make browsing through your enormous picture library easier and more fun.

Grouping Files That Get in the Way

Photoshop Elements has a feature called stacks that can help you organize and manage your files. Stacks are collections of photos that are grouped based on a common attribute, such as date, name, or visual similarity. You can create stacks manually or automatically, and you can expand or collapse them as needed. Stacks can help you reduce clutter, find photos faster, and compare similar shots. 📷 To create a stack manually, you can select the photos you want to group in the Organizer, and then choose Edit > Stack > Stack Selected Photos. To create a stack automatically, you can use the Auto-Stack by Capture Time option, which groups photos taken within a specified time interval. You can also use the Auto-Stack by Visual Similarity option, which groups photos that look alike. To access these options, choose Edit > Stack > Auto-Stack by Capture Time or Edit > Stack > Auto-Stack by Visual Similarity. To expand or collapse a stack, you can click the stack badge on the top-left corner of the thumbnail, or choose Edit > Stack > Expand Stack or Edit > Stack > Collapse Stack. You can also unstack photos by choosing Edit > Stack > Unstack Photos.

Marking files as hidden

The Hidden Files feature gives you more control over how your photos are organized. It's a strong tool that helps you organize your workspace more efficiently. With this function, you can choose which files in the organizer to show or conceal. This keeps everything organized and lets you concentrate on the items you want to work on. Crucially, hidden files are not removed from your computer; instead, they are not accessible via several functions, including slideshows, albums, searches, and more.

To utilize the Hidden Files feature, follow these steps:

Marking Files as Hidden:

1. **Select the Files:** Within the organizer, choose the files you want to hide.
2. **Hide Files**: Either select Edit > Hide Files or right-click and choose Hide Files from the context menu.
3. **Confirm Action:** A dialog box will prompt you to confirm your action. Click "Yes" to hide the selected files.

4. **Visual Indicator:** Hidden files will exhibit a dimmed appearance, accompanied by a crossed-out eye icon in the top-right corner of the thumbnail.

This process empowers you to reduce clutter, customizing your workspace to suit your current focus.

Revealing Hidden Files:

- **Access Hidden Files:** In the Organizer, choose View > Show Hidden Files or click the Show Hidden Files button located on the bottom-right corner of the window.
- **Visibility Restored:** Hidden files will become visible once again, and the crossed-out eye icon will disappear.

Unhidden Files:

- Select Files: Choose the files you want to unhide.
- Unhide Files: Either select Edit > Unhide Files or right-click and choose Unhide Files from the context menu.
- Confirm Action: A dialog box will appear, requesting confirmation. Click "Yes" to unhide the selected files.

Stackin' 'em up

Stacking is a feature designed to bring order to your growing collection of images in the Organizer. By grouping similar or related files together, you can minimize clutter and simplify your search processes. Whether you have multiple shots of the same scene, various edits of a single photo, or images belonging to a specific project, stacking provides a cohesive organizational solution. To create a stack, simply select the files you wish to group, right-click, and choose Stack > Stack Selected Photos. Easily expand or collapse a stack by clicking the icon on the top-left corner of the thumbnail. When it's time to disband a stack, right-click and choose Stack > Unstack Photos.

Creating versions

Creating versions allows you to safeguard different edits of the same file without altering the original, offering a versatile approach to experimentation and comparison. For instance, you can generate versions with distinct filters, effects, or adjustments while preserving the integrity of the initial file. To embark on this creative journey, open a file in the Photo Editor, introduce the desired changes, and navigate to File > Save As Version. This process ensures that your original file remains untouched, providing a convenient way to explore various artistic expressions. To manage and view your versions, seamlessly transition to the Organizer, select the file and click the Versions icon located on the bottom panel.

CHAPTER NINE

WORKING WITH CAMERA RAW EDITOR

Benefits of using Camera Raw Editor

The Camera Raw Editor is a powerful tool in Photoshop Elements 2024 that can elevate your picture editing to new levels. It offers a multitude of advantages and opens up new editing possibilities.

One of the standout advantages of the Camera Raw Editor is its non-destructive editing prowess. This means that every adjustment made to your photos occurs without altering the original image, preserving its pristine quality. This non-destructive approach offers the freedom to revert to the untouched original or explore diverse adjustments without compromising the integrity of your images. The assurance of maintaining quality throughout the editing process is a hallmark feature, providing a safety net for creative experimentation.

Efficiency meets precision with the Camera Raw Editor's ability to apply identical settings to multiple photos simultaneously. This time-saving feature not only streamlines your workflow but also ensures consistency across a series of images. The convenience of bulk editing empowers you to maintain a cohesive look and feel across your photo collection.

Venture into advanced editing terrain with the Camera Raw Editor, where a spectrum of sophisticated features awaits. Explore the intricacies of point color adjustments, delve into the art of lens blur to create captivating background effects, and venture into the realm of High Dynamic Range (HDR) output for stunning, detail-rich images.

These advanced tools open up new possibilities for refining colors, enhancing depth, and crafting visually striking compositions.

Compatibility is key, and the Camera Raw Editor seamlessly handles raw files from diverse cameras, as well as JPEG and TIFF files. This versatility ensures that, regardless of your preferred file format, you can extract the best possible results from your photos. The Camera Raw Editor's adaptability extends to a wide array of file types, making it a go-to solution for photographers working with various equipment.

The Camera Raw Editor emerges not only as a powerful editing tool but as a gateway to a realm where precision, efficiency, and creative exploration converge. Whether you're a seasoned photographer or an enthusiast, the Camera Raw Editor empowers you to transform your images with finesse and unlock their full potential.

Learning Different Raw File Formats

Explore the world of raw file formats to see the unfiltered jewels that your camera's sensor has caught and realize the full potential of your photography pursuits. Raw files provide photographers more freedom and control over their photographs than JPEG or TIFF formats do. This allows them to precisely edit their shots. Photoshop Elements 2024 offers a flexible framework that enables photographers to fully express their creativity by smoothly supporting a wide variety of raw file types from various camera models.

To navigate the intricacies of working with different raw file formats, follow these comprehensive steps:

Step 1: Install the Camera Raw Plugin

- Navigate to Help > Install Camera Raw in the Photoshop Elements Editor.

- This vital software plugin enables you to seamlessly open and edit raw files within the Photoshop Elements environment.

Step 2: Import Raw Files into the Organizer

- Access the organizer tool by going to File > Get Photos and Videos > From Files and Folders.
- Select the raw files you wish to import, initiating the organization process that lays the foundation for efficient workflow management.

Step 3: Open Raw Files in the Camera Raw Editor

- Highlight the raw files you want to edit within the organizer.
- Click on the Editor button located at the bottom of the screen, ushering you into the Camera Raw Editor.
- Within this powerful tool, exercise control over exposure, white balance, color, sharpness, noise, and various other settings to bring your vision to life.

Step 4: Save Edited Raw Files

- Navigate to the bottom of the Camera Raw Editor and click on the Save button.
- Choose the desired format (JPEG, TIFF, or PSD), set the quality parameters, and designate the location for your output files.
- This step ensures that your meticulously edited raw files are transformed into formats suitable for printing, sharing, or further refinement within Photoshop Elements.

Open your Photos in the Camera Raw Editor

Adobe Bridge is the entry point to begin processing raw photographs in Camera Raw. To go through the process with ease, adhere to these procedures:

1. **Open Raw Images:**
   - In Adobe Bridge, choose one or more raw camera files.
   - Choose File > Open in Camera Raw or press Ctrl+R (Windows) or Command+R (Mac OS).
   - After adjustments in the Camera Raw dialog box, click Done to accept changes or Open Image to open a copy in Photoshop.
2. **Processing JPEG or TIFF Images:**
   - Similarly, select JPEG or TIFF files in Adobe Bridge.
   - Choose File > Open in Camera Raw or use the shortcut keys.
   - Adjustments made can be accepted by clicking Done. Configure preferences for handling JPEG and TIFF images in the Camera Raw preferences.
3. **Importing Camera Raw Images in Photoshop:**
   - Select camera raw files in Adobe Bridge.
   - Choose File > Open With > Adobe Photoshop CS5 or use File > Open in Photoshop.
   - Adjustments in the Camera Raw dialog box can be applied by clicking Open Image. Press Alt (Windows) or Option (Mac OS) for a copy or Shift while clicking Open Image to open as a Smart Object.
4. **Tip for Adobe Bridge:**
   - Shift-double-click a thumbnail to open a camera raw image in Photoshop without the Camera Raw dialog box. Hold Shift while choosing File > Open to open multiple selected images.

Importing Camera Raw Images in After Effects:

Camera Raw offers a raw file processing mechanism for easy After Effects integration. Observe these recommendations:

1. **Importing Raw Files:**
   - In Adobe Bridge, choose one or more camera raw files.
   - Open the file using Adobe After Effects CS5 by selecting it. Adjustments made can be accepted by clicking OK.
2. **Importing TIFF and JPEG Files into After Effects:**
   - In After Effects, choose File > Import.
   - Choose All Files from the Enable menu (Mac OS) or Files of Type menu (Windows) in the Import File dialog box.
   - Select the file, choose Camera Raw from the Format menu, and click Open.
3. **Importing Camera Raw Images as a Sequence:**
   - Select File > Import in After Effects.
   - Select the images and choose the Camera Raw Sequence option. Click Open.
   - Settings from the first file are applied to the entire sequence unless an XMP sidecar file is present for subsequent frames.

Navigating Around the Camera Raw Editor Workspace

Camera Raw Editor Workspace shows itself as a powerful tool with a wide range of options to improve and enhance the quality of your raw photos. Take into account the following tips to efficiently traverse this feature-rich environment:

Initiating your journey with the Camera Raw Editor involves opening a raw image through the File menu, specifically by selecting File > Open and choosing the desired raw file from your computer. Alternatively, you can expedite this process by seamlessly dragging and dropping the file directly into the Photo Editor interface.

At the top of the Camera Raw Editor lies a comprehensive toolbar, equipped with an assortment of tools catering to various editing needs. From zooming and panning to cropping, rotating, straightening, healing, cloning, and implementing local adjustments, this toolbar empowers users with a versatile set of editing functionalities.

The right-hand side of the workspace hosts the histogram and basic adjustments panel, allowing users to make fundamental modifications to their images. Through an intuitive set of sliders, you can finely tune parameters such as exposure, contrast, color, clarity, detail, and more, shaping your image to perfection.

Exploring the basic adjustments panel unveils a wealth of options organized into different tabs. These tabs grant access to advanced features like curves, sharpening, noise reduction, lens corrections, effects, and presets, providing a comprehensive suite for meticulous image refinement.

To preview alterations in real time, simply toggle the Preview checkbox located at the top right corner of the Camera Raw Editor. This functionality enables you to assess and fine-tune your edits on the fly, ensuring a seamless and efficient editing process.

Comparing the original and edited versions of your image is facilitated through the Split View or Side-by-Side View buttons positioned at the bottom right corner of the Camera Raw Editor. These options allow for a detailed before-and-after examination, aiding in the evaluation of your editing decisions.

Once satisfied with your edits, saving the changes as a new file is achieved by clicking the Save Image button located at the bottom left corner of the Camera Raw Editor. This step ensures that your meticulously crafted adjustments are preserved in a distinct file.

To access the Photo Editor for more fine-tuning and improvements, just click the Open Image button located in the lower right corner of the Camera Raw Editor. Within the Photo Editor environment, this integrated workflow allows for a smooth transition from basic picture modifications to more complex editing operations.

Studying the Raw Editor Panels

Raw Editor Panels are an essential feature that can be accessed via the panel of basic adjustments on the right side of the large Camera Raw Editor Workspace. Accessible via these panels are a wide range of tools that allow you to carefully adjust tone, color, detail, geometry, and artistic effects among other aspects of your original picture.

In total, there are eight distinct panels, each distinguished by a unique icon and name, offering specialized functionalities to cater to diverse editing requirements:

1. **Basic Panel:** The Basic panel serves as a foundational hub, granting control over global adjustments such as exposure, contrast, white balance, vibrance, and saturation. This panel acts as the starting point for refining the overall visual appeal of your image.
2. **Tone Curve Panel:** The Tone Curve panel presents a sophisticated tool for modifying the tonal range and contrast within your image. Utilizing a curve graph, users can intricately sculpt the overall tonal

balance, providing nuanced control over the image's visual dynamics.

3. **Detail Panel:** Focused on precision, the Detail panel facilitates the sharpening and noise reduction processes within your image. Through an array of sliders and preview windows, users can meticulously enhance the clarity and sharpness while minimizing unwanted noise.

4. **Color Mixer Panel:** The Color Mixer panel is a palette for adjusting the hue, saturation, and luminance of individual color ranges in your image. This level of granular control empowers users to precisely manipulate the color composition, ensuring vibrant and balanced results.

5. **Color Grading Panel:** Introducing a nuanced approach to color adjustments, the Color Grading panel allows users to apply distinct color tints to the shadows, mid-tones, and highlights. Utilizing color wheels, this panel enhances the creative possibilities, adding a layer of sophistication to your imagery.

6. **Optics Panel:** The Optics panel addresses technical imperfections within your image, offering corrective tools for lens distortions, chromatic aberrations, and vignetting. Checkboxes and sliders facilitate seamless correction, ensuring optimal image quality.

7. **Geometry Panel:** The Geometry panel ventures into transformative territory, providing tools and grids for adjusting perspective, scale, rotation, and alignment. This panel is instrumental in rectifying distortions and aligning elements for a visually pleasing composition.

8. **Effects Panel:** Users may now add artistic aspects to their photographs with the Effects panel, opening them to a new creative environment. This panel increases the visual impact of your photos by using effects like post-crop vignettes and adding grain and texture.

It is simple to move between these panels by clicking on their icons or by using the keyboard keys that are provided underneath them. Additionally, users may create a more organized workplace by folding or extending panels, which provides a personalized editing experience. Through accurate and imaginative modifications, users can fully realize the potential of their raw photographs thanks to the Camera Raw Editor's well-thought-out panel integration.

Starting with the basic Panel

The basic Panel interface serves as the initial segment in the comprehensive Basic Adjustments panel located on the right side of the Camera Raw Editor Workspace. This tab provides a multitude of controls allowing users to finely tune global parameters such as exposure, contrast, white balance, vibrance, and saturation for their images.

To effectively utilize the Basic panel, adhere to the following steps:

1. Navigate to the Basic tab situated in the Basic Adjustments panel. Here, a set of sliders and buttons are presented, each corresponding to distinct attributes of your image.
2. Utilize the temperature and tint sliders to modify the color balance of your image. Additionally, leverage the White Balance button to

opt for preset options or employ the Eyedropper tool to sample a neutral color directly from your image.

3. Employ the exposure slider to alter the overall brightness of your image. Alternatively, utilize the Auto button to permit Photoshop Elements to autonomously adjust the exposure based on its analysis.
4. Employ the contrast slider to modify the distinction between light and dark regions within your image. Alternatively, make use of the Auto button to delegate the task of adjusting the contrast to Photoshop Elements.
5. Fine-tune the tonal range of your image by adjusting the Highlights, Shadows, Whites, and black sliders. For enhanced precision, hold down the Alt key (Windows) or Option key (Mac) while adjusting the sliders to visualize areas that may be clipped in your image.
6. Adjust the Vibrance and Saturation sliders to vary the intensity and purity of colors in your image. It's important to note that Vibrance impacts less saturated colors more prominently, while Saturation uniformly affects all colors.
7. Preview the alterations made to your image by clicking the Preview checkbox located at the top right corner of the Camera Raw Editor. Additionally, compare the original and modified versions of your image using the Split View or Side-by-Side View buttons situated at the bottom right corner of the Camera Raw Editor. This feature aids in comprehending the impact of adjustments applied.

Acquaint with the details and Calibration Panels

In Photoshop Element 2024, the Details and Calibration panels are two of the eight tabs within the basic adjustments panel located on the right side of the Camera Raw Editor Workspace. These panels allow users to finely adjust the sharpness, noise reduction, and color profile of their raw photographs.

Details Panel: This panel offers a variety of sliders and preview windows to enhance picture sharpness and control noise reduction. Sharpening helps distinguish edges and small features in the picture, while noise reduction smooths out graininess and speckles. Users can adjust settings for noise reduction, including smoothness, color, contrast, brightness, detail, and masking characteristics, as well as sliders for altering the sharpening parameters of quantity, radius, and detail. The zoom feature in the preview windows allows for a close examination of how edits have affected different parts of the picture.

Calibration Panel: This flexible tool uses sliders and a profile browser to adjust the color profile of the picture. A color profile serves as a set of guidelines to help Photoshop Elements understand and present the colors in the picture. Users have the option to create a custom profile by adjusting the hue, saturation, and luminance of the fundamental hues of red, green, and blue. Additionally, the panel allows for precise regulation of the overall color balance of the picture, as well as the ability to change the shadow tint, green primary, and blue primary. Whether creating a custom color profile or using a specified one, users can subtly modify the color of their photographs using the calibration panel.

Understanding Adobe Camera Raw Profile

An Adobe Camera Raw profile provides instructions on how to interpret and present the colors in your raw picture without any processing. An unprocessed file, a raw picture contains the information that your camera's sensor recorded. Using several profiles allows you to modify your image's looks without sacrificing the accuracy of the original data.

There are two different kinds of profiles: creative profiles and camera-matching profiles. Camera-matching profiles are carefully designed to replicate the color rendering of the standard, landscape, portrait, and other built-in image modes on your camera. These profiles are very helpful if you want to maintain the original look of your shot as it appears on the LCD screen of your camera. Conversely, creative profiles, which include choices like Vintage, Monochrome, Modern, and more, are made to incorporate a variety of artistic effects and moods into your picture. These profiles are a great resource for brainstorming ideas or boosting your image's emotional resonance.

Use the Profile Browser by doing the following actions to apply profiles in the Camera Raw Editor Workspace:

- By selecting File > Open and selecting the raw file from your computer, you may open a raw picture in the Camera Raw Editor. A different option is to just drag and drop the file into the Photo Editor window.
- Go to the Basic tab in the Camera Raw Editor's basic adjustments panel located on the right side. The Profile section is located at the top of the panel.
- Choose Browse from the dropdown menu by clicking on the Profile. When you take this step, the Profile Browser window will open and show you a range of categories and profiles to go over.
- Viewing the profiles within a category requires expanding it. To make the process of choosing a profile easier, make use of the Favorites, Recently Used, and Search options.

- To get a preview of a profile's effect on your picture, hover over it. To apply a profile, click on it, then use the Amount slider to change the intensity.
- Once you're happy, close the Profile Browser and go back to the Basic panel by clicking the Close button. You may also use the Menu symbol to access other choices, including Import Profiles or Manage Profiles, or use the Star icon to designate a profile as a favorite. Your ability to arrange and personalize your profile library is improved by these features.

Opening Non-Raw Images in the Camera Editor

Use the following easy procedures to work with and modify JPEG or TIFF files that are not raw pictures in the Camera Raw Editor:

Getting Single Non-Raw Image Opened:

- Choose File > Open As in the Photo Editor and choose your preferred non-raw file from your PC. You may also save time by just dragging and dropping the file into the Photo Editor window.
- Choose Camera Raw from the Format option in the resulting Open As dialog box, then click Open.
- The chosen non-raw picture opens in the Camera Raw Editor with ease, providing you with a panel and toolset that is the same as what is available for raw photographs.
- When you're done adjusting and enhancing the picture, click the Open Picture button in the lower right corner of the Camera Raw Editor to move it into the Photo Editor for more adjustments.

Accessing Multiple Non-Raw Pictures:

- To maximize productivity while working with many non-raw pictures, start the process by choosing each one in the Elements Organizer.
- To open the chosen non-raw photographs in the Camera Raw Editor interface at the same time, click File > Open in Camera Raw.

By following these instructions, users can be sure that the Camera Raw Editor's many tools and features are compatible with both raw and non-raw file formats, providing them with a consistent editing experience irrespective of the kind of file. Whether working with a single picture or several files, users may edit more quickly.

Converting and Saving Image

Photoshop Element offers a flexible technique for converting and storing photos, allowing you to choose several settings, such as file format, name, location, and image quality. A variety of commands, including Save, Save As, and Export As, are available in the program to meet different needs. It supports some file types, including JPEG, PNG, TIFF, PSD, GIF, JPEG 2000, JPEG XR, and SVG.

Converting and Saving an Image:

1. **Open the Image:**
    - Launch the Photo Editor and open your desired image using File > Open or by dragging and dropping the file into the interface.
2. **Save or Save As:**

- Select File > Save or File > Save As to initiate the Save As dialog box (Ctrl+Shift+S for Windows or Command+Shift+S for Mac OS).
- Specify a filename, choose a location, and decide whether to include the image in the Elements Organizer catalog or save it in a version set with the original image.

3. **Choose File Format:**
   - From the Format menu, opt for a file format (JPEG, PNG, TIFF, PSD, GIF).
   - Depending on the selected format, additional options like quality, compression, or color profile may appear.
4. **Save the Image:**
   - Click Save to store the image in the designated format and location.
   - Alternatively, choose Save As Copy to preserve a duplicate without closing the original file.

Exporting an Image

1. **Open the Image:**
   - Open the desired image in the Photo Editor using File > Open or by dragging and dropping the file.
2. **Export As:**
   - Click File > Export As or use the shortcut (Ctrl+Alt+Shift+W for Windows or Command+Option+Shift+W for Mac OS).
   - The Export As dialog box will appear.
3. **Choose File Format for Web Optimization:**
   - Pick a web-optimized file format from the Format menu (JPEG 2000, JPEG XR, or SVG).

4. **Adjust Format-Specific Settings:**
    - Put settings like quality, size, metadata, or color space based on the chosen format.
5. **Export the Image:**
    - Click Export to save the image in the specified format and location.
    - Alternatively, choose Export All to export all open images in the same format and location simultaneously.

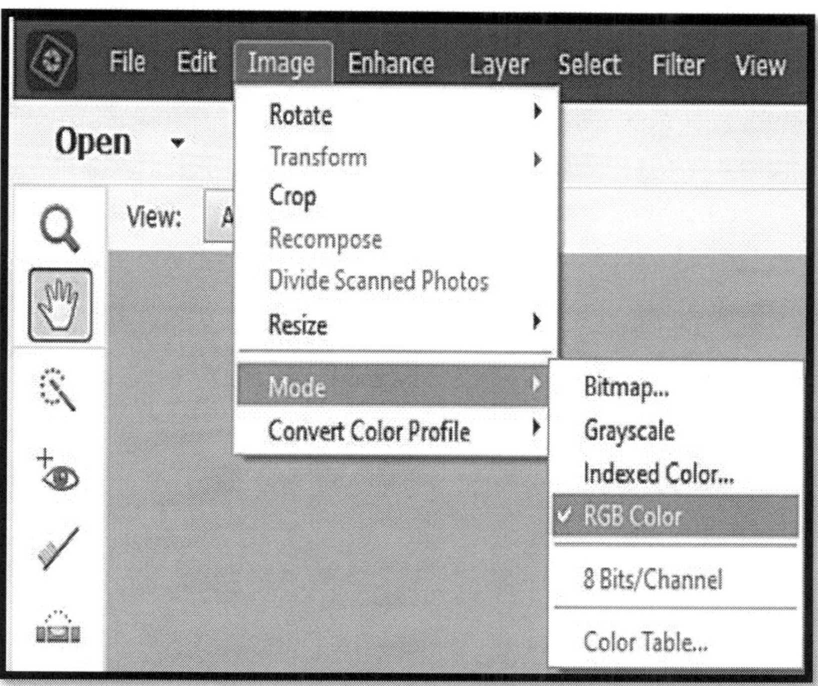

CHAPTER TEN

CREATING AND ADJUSTING A SELECTION

Creating a Selection

Use one of the selection tools in the Tools panel, such as the Quick Selection tool, the Lasso tool, or the Rectangular Marquee tool, to make a selection. The Tool Choices panel allows you to customize the many features and choices available for each tool. You may adjust your selection's aspect ratio, anti-aliasing, and feathering, for instance.

After a choice is made, a plethora of editing options becomes available. You may make exact alterations by using the chosen portion of your picture as a canvas to apply filters, tweaks, or transformations. After that, you may do things like copy, move, or delete the pixels that you have chosen. These pixels may also be easily placed into another picture, enabling the imaginative blending of various components.

The Refine Selection Brush tool is very useful for finer selection accuracy. This is a very useful tool for fine and precise selections, particularly when working with complicated edges such as those in grass, fur, or hair. Users may more accurately traverse the subtleties of difficult shapes by using the Refine Selection Brush.

Photoshop Element 2024 also offers the ability to utilize keyboard commands to further fine-tune choices. With the use of these instructions, users may modify, enlarge, or reduce the size of their current choices, providing a flexible and effective method for creating well-defined focal points in images. Because selection approaches are flexible, users may modify their approach according to the subtlety of the material, producing edits that are polished and well-refined.

Creating Rectangular and Elliptical Selection

Scroll to the toolbar and pick the Elliptical Marquee tool (M). If you are unable to locate the Elliptical Marquee tool, you can access a submenu of complementary tools by clicking and holding the Rectangular Marquee tool icon. Next, choose the Elliptical Marquee tool from the list of available choices.

After selecting the tool, use the choices in the options box to fine-tune your decision. Indicate which selection option you would want to use: add to an existing selection, subtract from an existing selection, intersect with another selection, or create a new one. You may dynamically customize how your selection evolves with these settings. Additionally, adjust the feathering for your choice in the settings bar. By softening the boundaries of your selection, feathering makes the transition between the regions that are chosen and those that are not more smoothly defined. You may also turn anti-aliasing on or off according to your preferences. By reducing the sharp edges in your selection, anti-aliasing helps to produce a refined final product. Choose the appropriate selection type, such as Normal, Fixed Ratio, or Fixed Size, based on the Elliptical Marquee tool's particular needs.

Click and drag within the picture to apply your selection by encircling the region you want to choose. For accuracy, you may limit your elliptical marquee to a perfect circle by holding down the Shift key and dragging it in any direction. As an alternative, you may create an elliptical selection that extends outward from the center by holding down the Alt (Windows) or Option (Mac) keys while dragging. This technique's adaptability gives you the ability to precisely customize your choices, guaranteeing that Photoshop Element 2024's Elliptical Marquee tool can handle a wide variety of editing settings.

Understanding Marquee Option

A marquee feature is a versatile tool that simplifies the process of selecting specific areas of your image using circular or rectangular shapes. It is crucial for various editing tasks such as copying, cropping, moving, and adjusting the selected area. Users can also modify the selection's size, shape, and feathering using keyboard shortcuts or the settings bar.

To use the marquee option effectively, access the tools panel and select one of the four marquee tools: single row, single column, rectangular, or elliptical marquee. Then, drag the chosen tool over the relevant area of your image. Holding down the Shift key will constrain the selection to a perfect square or circle for increased precision. Alternatively, you can specify precise dimensions for the selection using the fixed ratio or fixed size options.

While the marquee option is beneficial for selecting simple and precise elements in your image, other selection tools such as lasso tools or the quick selection tool may be more suitable for complex or asymmetrical shapes. Users can also explore the choose and mask workspace, which provides advanced features and controls to enhance selection accuracy.

The marquee feature enables you to make precise selections throughout the editing process, facilitating easier and more effective implementation of various modifications and additions in Photoshop Element. Regardless of the complexity of the chosen elements, the marquee tool is a fundamental component for a wide range of selection tasks.

Creating Freehand with Lasso Tools

Choose the Lasso tool located in the toolbox to initiate the selection process. Optionally, customize the Lasso tool settings by accessing the Tool Options bar. Next, employ the tool by dragging the cursor to create a freehand selection border according to your desired area.
To complete the selection, simply release the mouse button. If additional fine-tuning is necessary, consider clicking on the "Refine Edge" option. This will grant you access to advanced settings and adjustments, allowing you to refine and enhance the precision of your selection further. This comprehensive approach ensures a more accurate and tailored selection based on your specific requirements.

Understanding the Use of Cookie-Cutter Tool

The Cookie Cutter tool offers a creative way to customize your photos by cropping them into unique shapes of your choice. In Expert mode, access the tool by selecting the Crop tool.

Navigate to the Tool Options panel and click on the Cookie Cutter icon. Choose a shape from the available options. Explore different shape libraries by selecting a specific one from the Shapes drop-down menu.

Upon selecting a shape, double-click to confirm your choice. Drag the shape onto your photo, establishing the shape boundary. Easily manipulate the size and position of the bounding box to precisely capture the desired area for cropping.

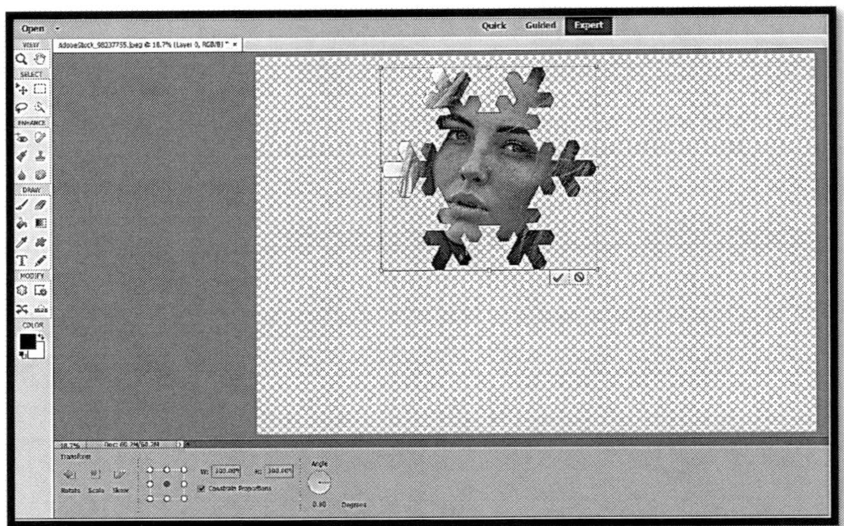

Click the Commit button or press Enter to finalize the cropping process. If you need to abort the operation, click the Cancel button or press Esc. Elevate your photo editing experience by using the Cookie Cutter tool to impart a touch of creativity and fun to your images.

Working with the Eraser Tool

The Eraser Tool

The Eraser tool in Photoshop Elements offers a unique approach to image editing by applying the background color, despite its name suggesting pixel transparency. Instead of creating transparent pixels, it replaces them with the chosen background color, as opposed to the foreground color. Utilizing the Eraser Tool involves several steps to ensure precision in color application.

To commence, locate the "Eraser Tool" button in the Toolbox and, if needed, access the Tool Options Bar. Set the color to be applied as the "Background" color in the Toolbox. It is imperative to select the appropriate layer in the "Layers" panel to ensure the selected color is applied to the desired layer.

Within the Tool Options Bar, customize your eraser by selecting a shape from the "Brush Preset Picker" pop-up menu. Adjust the eraser tip width using the "Size" slider for further control. The "Type" section in the Tool Options Bar allows you to choose between "Brush," "Pencil," or "Block" settings for the eraser.

If opting for "Brush" or "Pencil" as the eraser type, fine-tune the transparency level using the "Opacity" slider. Once the desired settings are in place, click and drag in the photo to apply the background color, effectively erasing pixels based on the current configurations.

Background Eraser Tool

To employ the Eraser Tool in Photoshop Elements, initiate the process by clicking on the "Eraser Tool" button located in the Toolbox, and if needed, navigate to the Tool Options Bar. Following this, designate the color to be applied by selecting the "Background" color in the Toolbox.

Next, ensure the accuracy of the color application by choosing the appropriate layer in the "Layers" panel. Fine-tune the eraser's characteristics by opting for a specific shape from the "Brush Preset Picker" pop-up menu within the Tool Options Bar.

Refine the eraser tip's width using the "Size" slider, and in the "Type" section of the Tool Options Bar, make a selection between "Brush," "Pencil," or "Block" settings for the eraser. If the chosen "Type" is "Brush" or "Pencil," regulate the transparency level of the applied color using the "Opacity" slider.

To execute the erasing action with the configured settings, simply click and drag within the photo, applying the current background color seamlessly. This comprehensive approach ensures precise and customized utilization of the Eraser Tool in Photoshop Elements for effective image editing.

The Magic Eraser Tool

Magic Eraser Tool can be used to easily edit consistent pixels across a picture. Using this tool on a layer that has manually locked transparent pixels will cause the selected pixels to become the color of the backdrop rather than being erased to transparency. This also holds for a "Background" layer, which, when using the Magic Eraser Tool, is transformed into a standard layer.

With this tool, you can choose to remove all pixels that have the same color or only continuous pixels—that is, pixels that are next to each other. This feature improves the Magic Eraser Tool's accuracy and adaptability by enabling smooth modifications to certain regions while retaining control over pixel transformations in various layer contexts.

To employ the Magic Eraser Tool in Photoshop Elements, begin by selecting it from the Toolbox. Ensure that the tool is also activated within the Tool Options Bar, if necessary. Notably, it shares a button in the Toolbox with the Eraser Tool and Background Eraser Tool.

Specify the range of colors to be removed by utilizing the "Tolerance" slider in the Tool Options Bar. A low tolerance erases pixels with a color very closely resembling the selected one, while a higher tolerance broadens the range of color similarity for erasure.

Fine-tune the opacity of the erased pixels using the "Opacity" slider. A 100% opacity completely removes all selected pixels, whereas lower opacity levels result in partial erasure. To achieve smooth edges instead of jagged ones in the erased selection, activate the "Anti-aliasing" checkbox.

For more precise erasing, utilize the "Contiguous" checkbox to restrict erasure to pixels directly touching the selected color. If unchecked, all pixels of the chosen color anywhere in the image will be erased. To sample the color for erasure using combined data from all visible layers, check the "Sample All Layers" checkbox.

To execute the erasure with the configured settings, select the layer containing the pixels to be erased from the Layers panel. Click on the pixel color in the chosen layer within the image to initiate the erasure process. This comprehensive approach ensures effective utilization of the Magic Eraser Tool while providing control over various erasure parameters in Photoshop Elements.

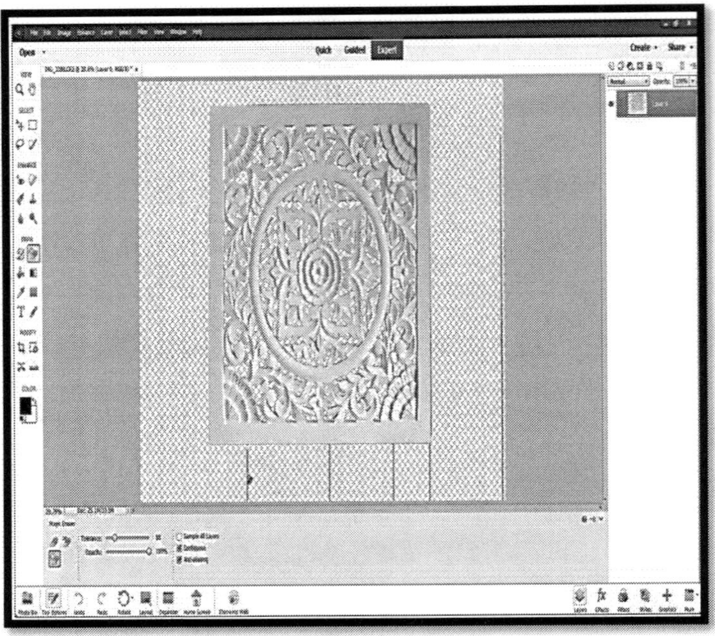

Feathering a Selection

Feathering serves as a technique to gently blur the sharp boundaries of an object within your image. This process involves a gradual transition between the colors of the pixels at the object's edge and those in its immediate surroundings. The purpose of feathering extends beyond seamlessly integrating a newly added element into the overall image; it also fulfills various other reasons for softening edges within your creative composition.

Step 1: Selection Process: Initiate the feathering process by meticulously selecting the area using a suitable selection tool, such as the Quick Selection tool. This initial step ensures precision in identifying the specific region where the feathering effect will be applied.

Step 2: Masking Configuration: Proceed to refine the selection by opting for the Select and Mask feature accessible from the options bar.

This tool provides a platform for fine-tuning the boundaries of your selection, setting the stage for seamless integration of the feathering effect.

Step 3: Feathering Adjustment: Navigate to the Properties panel situated on the right side of the screen. Within this panel, utilize the Feather slider to modulate the degree of blur applied to the layer mask overlaying the selected area. This dynamic control allows you to tailor the feathering effect to achieve the desired level of softness around the edges.

Step 4: Application Confirmation: Once satisfied with the configured feathering settings, confirm your adjustments by clicking the OK button. This action solidifies the application of the feathering effect to the selected area, seamlessly blending it with the surrounding elements in your composition.

Step 5: Copy and Paste Integration: If the need arises to replicate or transfer the feathered mask to another layer, execute the copy-and-paste procedure. Press Ctrl+C (Command+C on Mac) to copy the mask and Ctrl+V (Command+V on Mac) to paste it onto the desired layer. This versatile maneuver allows you to extend the feathering effect to different elements within your project, ensuring a cohesive and harmonious visual result.

Save and Load Selection Commands

Preserving a chosen area in a photo for future edits is facilitated through the process of saving a selection. This enables you to focus on other aspects of the photo before ultimately reloading the saved selection.

Here's a step-by-step guide:

1. In the Edit workspace, create a selection in your photo using the available tools.
2. Navigate to Select > Save Selection.
3. In the ensuing Save Selection dialog box, opt for "New" from the Selection pop-up menu.
4. Provide a name for the selection in the Name box and proceed by clicking the OK button.

To reload the saved selection:

- Choose Select > Load Selection.
- Within the Load Selection dialog box, select the saved selection from the Selection menu.
- Confirm your choice by clicking the OK button.

For deletion of a selection:

- Choose Select > Delete Selection.
- In the subsequent dialog box, pick a saved selection from the Selection menu.

5. Finalize the deletion process by clicking OK.

Refining the Edges of Your Selection

Utilizing different Selection Brushes, you may adjust your choices more precisely inside the Tool Options. Selecting a brush and then selecting "Add to selection" or "Subtract from selection" will allow you to modify the selection by adding or removing regions.

You may also use the "Select > Refine Edge" option for a more accurate modification. You may access sophisticated refining tools and controls with this function, which lets you further improve your choices. The Refine Edge feature offers a flexible and thorough way to refine your choices, whether you need to add minute details or remove undesired components.

CHAPTER ELEVEN

GETTING STARTED WITH LAYERS

Studying the Layers Panel

The Layers panel serves as a fundamental tool for effectively managing different components within an image. Its versatile functionalities enable the creation, modification, organization, and merging of layers, facilitating the achievement of diverse visual effects.

Accessing the Layers panel can be accomplished either by navigating to Window > Layers or by clicking the Layers icon in the taskbar. This comprehensive panel displays all layers within your image, ranging from the topmost layer to the background layer at the bottom. The active layer, denoting the currently edited layer, is highlighted in blue, and switching to another layer is as simple as clicking on it.

The Layers panel's icons and menus may be used to perform a wide range of activities on layers, including:

1. **Create a New Layer:** Initiate a new layer by clicking the "Create a new layer" icon at the panel's bottom or by opting for Layer > New > Layer.
2. **Delete a Layer:** Remove a layer by dragging it to the trash icon at the panel's bottom or by selecting Layer > Delete > Layer.
3. **Change Visibility:** Toggle the visibility of a layer by clicking the eye icon next to the layer thumbnail or by using Layer > Hide/Show Layer.
4. **Adjust Opacity:** Modify a layer's opacity by either dragging the opacity slider at the panel's top or inputting a specific value in the designated box.

5. **Blend Modes:** Alter a layer's blending mode by selecting an option from the Mode menu at the panel's top. The blending mode determines how the layer's pixels interact with those beneath it.
6. **Reorder Layers:** Rearrange layers by dragging them up or down in the panel or by choosing Layer > Arrange > Bring to Front/Back/Send Backward/Bring Forward.
7. **Link or Unlink Layers:** Connect or disconnect layers by clicking the link icon next to the layer thumbnail or by opting for Layer > Link/Unlink Layers. Linking layers facilitates simultaneous movement, transformation, or filter application to multiple layers.
8. **Lock or Unlock Layers:** Secure or release layers by clicking the lock icon next to the layer thumbnail or by choosing Layer > Lock/Unlock Layers. Locking prevents any alterations to the layer.
9. Merge Layers: Combine layers into a single entity by choosing Layer > Merge > Merge Down/Merge Visible/Merge Linked/Flatten Image. Merging reduces file size and simplifies the image by consolidating layers.

Converting the Background to a Layer

Follow these procedures to convert the background layer to a regular layer:

1. **Access the Background Layer:**
    - Either double-click on the "Background" in the Layers panel.
    - Alternatively, navigate to the menu and select Layer > New > Layer From Background.
2. **Configure Layer Options:**
    - Once the background layer is activated, set specific layer options according to your requirements. Refer to the

guidelines on creating layers and groups for detailed customization.

3. **Confirmation:**
   - After adjusting the layer options, confirm the changes by selecting "OK.

Understanding the Layer Menu and Layer Panel Menu

Photoshop Elements gives users flexible tools for layer management and creativity by providing access to a multitude of commands and choices for modifying layers via either the Layer menu or the Layer panel menu.

Layer Menu: Situated in the menu bar at the top of the screen, the Layer menu serves as a comprehensive center for various layer-related actions. Within this menu, you can find commands for creating, deleting, arranging, merging, locking, linking, and transforming layers. Additionally, it provides options for generating adjustment layers, fill layers, type layers, and shape layers. The Layer menu becomes a powerful tool for applying layer styles, layer masks, and smart filters to enhance the visual impact of your layers.

Layer Panel Menu: Nestled in the upper-right corner of the Layers panel, the Layer panel menu shares some commands with the Layer menu while offering additional features customized for managing the Layers panel itself. This menu becomes particularly handy for tasks like changing the panel view, sorting layers by name or type, duplicating or deleting layers, and creating layer groups or layer comps. It provides a more localized and panel-centric approach to layer management.

Both the Layer menu and the Layer Panel menu operate in a context-sensitive manner. This means that the available commands and options adapt based on the type and quantity of layers you have selected. For instance, selecting a type layer will reveal commands related to text editing and formatting, while choosing multiple layers will expose commands pertinent to aligning and distributing layers.

Understanding Select Menus

The Select menu serves as an essential resource for crafting, refining, and managing selections within your images. Conveniently located in the menu bar at the top of the screen, this menu offers a comprehensive array of commands to enhance your selection process.

Selection Creation and Modification: Within the Select menu, you'll find commands for creating, modifying, saving, and loading selections. Whether you need to encompass all pixels in your image or selectively target pixels based on color, brightness, or similarity, the Select menu provides the tools you need. You can precisely manipulate selection edges using commands like invert, expand, contract, feather, smooth, or refine.

Integration with Selection Tools: The Select menu seamlessly collaborates with the selection tools housed in the Tools panel, including the Marquee, Lasso, Quick Selection, and Magic Wand tools. These tools empower you to draw or click on specific areas within your image that you wish to select. Once your initial selection is made using these tools, the Select menu steps in to offer additional refinements, allowing you to fine-tune and perfect your selection with ease.

Enhanced Selection Control: The Select menu acts as a centralized command center to augment the capabilities of selection tools, providing you with unparalleled control over the selection process. Whether you're creating intricate masks, isolating specific elements, or performing complex adjustments, the Select menu becomes an indispensable support in achieving precision and accuracy.

Understanding Different Types of Layer

Layers function like a series of transparent sheets, each stacked upon the other, allowing you to paint images, apply effects, or insert text and shapes. The transparency of each layer enables a view through to the layers beneath, providing a versatile canvas for creative exploration.

The Image Layer

This is the most common layer, housing pixel-based (raster) images such as photographs, drawings, or scanned artwork. Image layers permit actions like painting, erasing, cloning, filtering, or transforming. Additionally, you can make adjustments to color, brightness, contrast, and other properties. The background layer, a specialized image layer, is always locked and situated at the bottom of the layer stack.

The Adjustment Layers

This type of layer allows for the application of color or tonal adjustments without permanently altering the pixels. Adjustments to brightness, contrast, hue, saturation, or color balance are possible, and the use of masks enables targeting specific areas of the image. Adjustment layers are non-destructive, providing the flexibility to edit or delete them at any time.

The Fill Layers

Filled with a solid color, gradient, or pattern, this layer type is ideal for creating backgrounds, adding color effects, or filling selections with textures. Like adjustment layers, fill layers are non-destructive, allowing for easy editing or deletion, and masks can be employed to limit their impact on specific areas of the image.

The Shape Layers

This layer contains vector-based shapes, such as rectangles, ellipses, stars, or custom designs. Valuable for crafting logos, icons, buttons, or other graphics, shape layers support the application of layer styles like drop shadows, glows, or bevels. As with other non-destructive layers, shape layers can be edited or deleted at any point.

The Type Layer

Housing vector-based text, this layer type is perfect for adding captions, titles, labels, or other textual elements to your image. Similar to shape layers, type layers support layer styles for further customization and are non-destructive, allowing for easy edits or removal.

Photoshop Elements offers a simpler method for managing layers using the Layers panel, Layer menu, or Layer panel menu. In addition to generating and altering layers, you may group and combine them, manipulating attributes like opacity, visibility, blending mode, order, and locking to get the intended aesthetic effect. With such a wide range of layer types and features, users may let their imaginations run wild and yet have the freedom to make any adjustments at any point throughout the creation process.

Creating a New Layer from the Scratch

To create a new layer from scratch you can follow these steps:

- Open the image you want to work on in the Photo Editor workspace.
- In the Layers panel, click the Create a new layer icon at the bottom of the panel. Alternatively, you can choose Layer > New > Layer from the menu bar.
- A new layer will appear above the active layer in the Layers panel. The new layer will have a default name, such as Layer 1, and will be transparent.
- To rename the new layer, double-click it and type a new name. Press Enter to confirm.
- To change the opacity, blending mode, or visibility of the new layer, use the options at the top of the Layers panel.
- To add content to the new layer, you can use any of the tools in the Tools panel, such as the Brush, Eraser, Text, or Shape tools. You can also paste an image or a selection from another layer onto the new layer.

Creating Layer with Layer via Copy and Layer via Cut Commands

Utilizing the Layer via Copy and Layer via Cut commands provides an efficient means to generate new layers based on existing ones.

The Layer via Copy command facilitates the creation of a new layer by duplicating the selected pixels from the active layer, leaving the original layer untouched. This command proves invaluable for replicating specific portions of an image or generating variations of the same element.

On the other hand, the Layer via Cut command not only produces a new layer with the selected pixels but also removes them from the original layer, rendering the selected area transparent. This command is particularly useful for isolating elements within an image or relocating them to different positions.

To employ the Layer via Copy or Layer via Cut commands, you can follow these step-by-step instructions:

1. Open the desired image in the Photo Editor workspace.
2. In the Layers panel, ensure that the layer containing the pixels you intend to copy or cut is selected, and confirm that the layer is neither locked nor hidden.
3. Utilize any of the selection tools available in the Tools panel, such as Marquee, Lasso, Quick Selection, or Magic Wand, to highlight the pixels you want to copy or cut.
4. Navigate to the menu bar and select Layer > New > Layer via Copy or Layer via Cut. Alternatively, you can employ the keyboard shortcuts Ctrl+J (Windows) or Command+J (Mac) for Layer via Copy, or Ctrl+Shift+J (Windows) or Command+Shift+J (Mac) for Layer via Cut.
5. A new layer will materialize above the active layer in the Layers panel, adorned with a default name like "Layer 1 copy," containing the selected pixels. You have the flexibility to rename the new layer by double-clicking it and entering a new name, confirming with the Enter key.
6. To refine the new layer, unleash the array of tools or commands available in the Tools panel, Layer menu, or Layer panel menu. This allows you to perform actions such as moving, transforming, filtering, or adjusting the new layer to achieve the desired effect.

Creating Layer Using Drag and Drop Method

The drag-and-drop technique makes layer creation simple and provides a smooth approach to combining parts from one picture with another. For a hassle-free experience, adhere to these guidelines:

1. Begin by opening the images you wish to work with in the Photo Editor workspace.
2. Within the Photo Bin, select the image that houses the specific element you intend to transfer to another image. Ensure that this source image is neither locked nor hidden.
3. Utilize any of the versatile selection tools located in the Tools panel—options include the Marquee, Lasso, Quick Selection, or Magic Wand tools—to precisely highlight the element you wish to copy.
4. Execute a drag-and-drop action, moving the selected element from the Photo Bin to the image window where you want to integrate it. This action automatically triggers the creation of a new layer in the target image, featuring the copied element. To personalize this new layer, simply double-click its name in the Layers panel, input a new name, and press Enter to confirm the change.
5. Enhance the flexibility of the new layer by leveraging the diverse set of tools and commands available in the Tools panel, Layer menu, or Layer panel menu. This allows for an array of modifications, including movement, transformation, filtering, or adjustments to the layer's appearance.

Transforming your Layers

By using the Transform or Free Transform commands, you can easily unlock the transforming power of your layers. You may use these instructions as a flexible toolbox to realize your creative vision by resizing, rotating, shifting, flipping, or distorting your layers.

The Transform command extends a range of predefined transformations at your fingertips, including scale, rotate, skew, distort, perspective, and warp. Numeric values for these transformations can be precisely entered in the Tool Options panel, offering meticulous control over the adjustment process.
Conversely, the Free Transform command grants you the freedom to intuitively manipulate your layer by dragging handles within a bounding box. This dynamic method permits any form of transformation with ease. Furthermore, keyboard modifiers add an extra layer of control, enabling you to constrain or fine-tune your transformations.

To harness the power of the Transform or Free Transform commands, adhere to these steps:

1. Open your desired image within the Photo Editor workspace.
2. In the Layers panel, ensure the selected layers are neither locked nor hidden.
3. Navigate to the menu bar and select Image > Transform or Image > Free Transform. Alternatively, you can use keyboard shortcuts like Ctrl+T (Windows) or Command+T (Mac) for Free Transform, or Ctrl+Shift+T (Windows) or Command+Shift+T (Mac) for Transform.
4. If opting for Transform, select a specific transformation from the Tool Options panel, such as Scale, Rotate, or Skew. Adjust numeric values to fine-tune the transformation or drag the bounding box handles for a visual adjustment.

5. If choosing Free Transform, manipulate the bounding box handles to achieve your desired transformation. Employ keyboard modifiers for additional control:
    - Shift: Constrain proportions or angles.
    - Alt (Windows) or Option (Mac): Transform from the center or duplicate the layer.
    - Ctrl (Windows) or Command (Mac): Distort or warp the layer.
    - Ctrl+Alt (Windows) or Command+Option (Mac): Apply perspective transformations.
6. Confirm the transformation by pressing Enter or clicking the green check mark icon in the Tool Options panel. To cancel the transformation, press Esc or click the red cross icon in the Tool Options panel.

Adding a Layer Mask

A layer mask is a flexible tool that allows you to manage which areas of a layer are shown. This dynamic feature makes it possible to reveal or hide parts of a picture, which makes it easier to create smooth transparency gradients. To include a layer mask into your artwork in a smooth manner, take note of these detailed steps:

- First, open the Layers panel and choose the layer you want to mask by highlighting the specific element you want to mask.
- Select the Quick Selection Tool from the tools panel on the left. With this tool, you can precisely manage the masking process by designating the areas of the picture that you wish to expose.
- Use the Quick Selection Tool to choose the area of the picture that you want to display by drawing over it. Make sure the selection is limited to this region. Holding down the Alt key as

you click will allow you to refine the selection by eliminating unnecessary parts and focusing just on the particular elements you want to draw attention to.

- The Add Layer Mask icon is located on the right side of the Layers panel; pay attention to it. This icon may be clicked to start the layer mask-generating process. After that, in the Layers panel, a layer mask thumbnail will show up next to the layer thumbnail. The visible regions are shown in white on this thumbnail, while the sections that are hidden are shown in black.
- Choose the thumbnail of the layer mask to delve into its details. In this step, the Brush tool becomes your ally. Use this tool to paint the layer mask in black or white. Certain areas of the layer are visible in white, while others are hidden in black. The dynamic painting technique enables you to adjust the mask to your vision.
- You may use the Eraser tool to selectively delete portions of the mask if accuracy is required. This gives you much more control over the regions that are hidden, enabling you to make precise alterations.

Flattening Layers

Flattening layers involves merging all visible layers in your image into a unified background layer. This process offers advantages such as reducing file size and enhancing image editing performance. However, it comes with trade-offs, as flattening means forfeiting the ability to edit individual layers. This step should be taken only when you are satisfied with your final composition or when preparing the image for printing or sharing. Here's a detailed exploration of the benefits and drawbacks of flattening layers:

Benefits:

1. **File Size Reduction**: Flattening layers significantly decreases the file size, facilitating easier storage, transfer, and opening of your images.
2. **Performance Improvement**: With fewer layers to process, image editing performance is optimized, leading to a smoother and more responsive workflow.
3. **Editing Efficiency:** Certain editing processes, such as applying filters, adjustments, or transformations, can be more efficiently executed with a single, flattened layer.

Drawbacks:

1. **Loss of Editability**: Flattening layers means relinquishing the ability to individually undo, modify, or rearrange them later.
2. **Loss of Transparency and Blending Modes:** The transparency and blending modes of each layer are forfeited, limiting the creation of complex effects or intricate compositions.
3. **Irreversibility:** Once layers are flattened, the process is irreversible, and the original layers cannot be restored.

Before proceeding with layer flattening, take the following precautions:

- **Create Backups:** Ensure you have a backup copy of your image or save it with a different file name to preserve the original layers.

- **Finalize Edits:** Confirm that all desired changes and corrections have been applied to the layers and that there is no further need for individual layer edits.

To flatten layers follow these steps:

1. **Select Layer**: Choose the layer you wish to flatten in the Layers panel on the right side of the screen.
2. **Flatten Image:** Opt for either "Layer > Flatten Image" from the top menu bar or right-click on any layer and select "Flatten Image" from the pop-up menu.
3. **Confirmation:** Confirm the flattening action by clicking "OK" in the dialog box that appears.

Merging Layers

Merging layers is a strategic process that involves combining multiple layers into a unified composition. This method serves various purposes, including reducing file size, simplifying the editing workflow, and introducing captivating effects to your images. The software provides diverse approaches to merging layers, offering flexibility and creative control. Here are distinct methods for merging layers:

1. Merge Down:

- **Description:** Merging the selected layer with the one immediately below it.
- **Shortcut:** Ctrl+E (Windows) or Command+E (Mac).

2. Merge Visible:

- **Description:** Merging all visible layers into a singular composition.

- **Shortcut**: Shift+Ctrl+E (Windows) or Shift+Command+E (Mac).

3. Merge Linked:

- **Description**: Merging layers that are linked together. Linking layers is achieved by clicking the link icon at the bottom of the Layers panel.
- **Procedure:** Link the desired layers before using a merging command.

4. Flatten Image:

- **Description:** Merging all layers into a consolidated background layer.
- **Shortcut:** Ctrl+Shift+F (Windows) or Command+Shift+F (Mac).

Each method has its distinct application and utility in the editing process. Here's a more detailed exploration of the individual methods:

- **Merge Down:** This method proves handy when you want to consolidate a specific layer with the one immediately beneath it. It's useful for streamlining the layer stack without affecting the visibility of other layers.
- **Merge Visible:** When dealing with multiple layers and seeking a comprehensive merge, especially for visible elements, this option is valuable. It streamlines the composition by combining all visible layers into a cohesive whole.
- **Merge Linked:** Useful for merging layers that are intentionally linked together for specific design or organizational purposes. Linking layers ensures they move and transform together.
- **Flatten Image:** If you aim to amalgamate all layers into a singular background layer, this method is apt. It's particularly

effective when preparing the image for printing or sharing, as it reduces the file size.

CHAPTER TWELVE

CREATING SIMPLE MAKEOVER

Cropping out Immaterial Parts from Image

Cropping serves as a powerful technique for eliminating extraneous elements and enhancing the focus of your photos. By utilizing the crop tool, you can precisely select the areas to retain, discarding the unnecessary parts. Here's a comprehensive guide on how to crop an image.

- Open the image you wish to edit.
- Select the crop tool from the toolbar. It typically resembles a square with a diagonal line.
- Drag the corners or sides of the crop box to define the size and shape of the area you want to retain. Alternatively, choose a preset aspect ratio from the drop-down menu on the left of the options bar for precision.
- If needed, rotate the crop box by moving the cursor outside the box and dragging when a curved arrow appears. Alternatively, enter a specific angle in the options bar for precise adjustments.
- To reposition the crop box, click inside it and drag it to a new location. Utilize the arrow keys for subtle adjustments.
- Once satisfied with the crop, click the green checkmark button on the right of the options bar. Alternatively, press Enter or double-click inside the box to apply the crop.
- To discard the changes and cancel the crop, click the red cross button on the right of the options bar or press Esc.

- Another method involves making a selection first. Choose the desired area, and then go to Image > Crop from the menu. This trims the image precisely to the bounding box containing the selection.

Straighten a Slanting Image

Correcting the alignment of a slanting image is an essential step in refining the visual appeal of your photographs. To achieve this, the software provides various tools, including the Straighten tool, Crop tool, and Ruler tool. Each tool serves a distinct purpose in rectifying image alignment. Here's an in-depth exploration of each tool:

1. **Straighten Tool within the Crop Tool:** The Straighten tool is seamlessly integrated into the Crop tool, offering a user-friendly method to align your image. Begin by selecting the Crop tool and locating the Straighten icon in the options bar. With this tool activated, you can draw a reference line along any straight edge within your image. Subsequently, the image will automatically rotate to align with the drawn line, ensuring a level composition.
2. **Manual Rotation with the Crop Tool**: The Crop tool provides additional flexibility by allowing manual rotation of the image. Simply drag the corners or sides of the crop box to adjust the orientation. The options bar displays the precise angle of rotation, enabling you to fine-tune the alignment according to your preferences. Moreover, you can opt for preset aspect ratios or input a custom one to further refine the cropping process.
3. **Ruler Tool for Measurement and Straightening:** The Ruler tool serves as a distinct entity, offering a comprehensive approach to

both measurement and straightening. Access this tool from the toolbar or use the keyboard shortcut 'I.' Once activated, draw a line along a straight edge within the image. Following this, navigate to Edit > Transform > Straighten Layer, triggering a rotation that aligns the image with the drawn line. This method is particularly useful for precise alignment adjustments based on specific measurements.

Reconstructing Images with Recompose Tool

Reconstructing images through the utilization of the Recompose tool presents a powerful method for resizing photos while preserving crucial visual elements like people, structures, animals, and more. This versatile tool serves a dual purpose, allowing users to eliminate unwanted or less significant areas from their images and alter the overall aspect ratio or orientation. The Recompose tool operates intelligently, dynamically adjusting pixels based on the areas designated for protection or removal.

To effectively employ the Recompose tool, follow these step-by-step instructions:

1. **Open Image and Access Recompose Tool:** Initiate the process by opening your image. Navigate to the toolbar and select the Recompose tool, or opt for the alternative method by choosing Image > Recompose from the menu bar.
2. **Mark Protected Areas with Protect Brush:** Utilize the Protect brush to mark areas within the image that you want to safeguard from alterations. The tool offers both Normal Highlight mode and Quick Highlight mode for this purpose, with green highlighting denoting the designated areas under protection.

3. **Identify and Remove Unwanted Areas with Remove Brush:** Employ the Remove brush to identify and mark areas in the image that you wish to eliminate or reduce. Red highlighting signifies the regions marked for removal, allowing for a precise and targeted adjustment.
4. **Adjust Image Size and Composition:** Choose from the available options to drag image handles or select a predefined size from the Preset drop-down menu. This step facilitates the decomposition process, resizing the image while intelligently filling in or removing pixels based on the protected or removed areas.
5. **Apply Recomposition or Cancel:** Once satisfied with the adjustments, click the green checkmark button to apply the recomposition. Alternatively, if changes are not to your liking, use the red cross button to cancel the recomposition, ensuring that the original state of the image is retained.

Using the Auto Fixes Commands

The Auto Fixes commands constitute a comprehensive set of options designed to swiftly enhance the color, contrast, lighting, and sharpness of your images. These commands are conveniently accessible through the Enhance menu or the Quick Actions panel within the Quick workspace. Let's delve into each Auto Fixes command:

Auto Smart Tone

The intelligent Adjustment feature offers an advanced way to improve the contrast and brightness of your images. This feature's foundation is an innovative algorithm that assesses the picture intelligently and makes minor tweaks to maximize visual attractiveness. This command is unique in that it allows users to fine-tune the image directly using a joystick interface, giving them exact control.

Using the Intelligent Adjustment command gives users the freedom to customize the outcomes to suit their tastes. Joystick control is a user-friendly and responsive instrument that enables dynamic changes to contrast and brightness characteristics. This interactive feature guarantees a hands-on editing experience by enabling users to precisely adjust the image's visual attributes.

Moreover, depending on user engagements, the Intelligent Adjustment command changes over time. The system learns and adjusts to different editing styles and preferences with each usage. Over time, the command provides more accurate and customized adjustments due to its adaptive learning process. The more times you use the Intelligent Adjustment command, the more proficient it becomes at matching your unique style preferences and making more customized adjustment suggestions for subsequent shots.

Auto Smart Fix

This intelligent correction applies adjustments to the overall appearance of your image, enhancing exposure, contrast, saturation, and color balance. Auto Smart Fix is tailored to provide a nuanced improvement to the visual appeal of your photograph.

Auto Level

Focusing on the tonal range, Auto Levels optimizes your image by setting black point, white point, and mid-tone values. This adjustment significantly enhances contrast and brightness, contributing to an overall improvement in image quality

Auto Contrast

This command uses highlight and shadow clipping to fine-tune contrast while enhancing picture sharpness and clarity. The end effect is a more defined and visually crisp look.

Auto Haze Removal

The Haze Removal command becomes a useful tool for reducing haze or fog in your photos so that they have a crisper, more colorful appearance. This specific function works particularly well on landscape photographs with far-off objects since haze often hides features and lessens overall clarity in these types of images.

Essentially, the Haze Removal command uses sophisticated algorithms to eliminate atmospheric interference in a picture just in certain areas, such as haze or fog. In doing so, it improves the visibility of far-off features, bringing to light minute details and making the picture sharper overall. This function works especially well for settings where the atmosphere may partly obscure far-off mountains, buildings, or natural features.

The Haze Removal command works well since it may enhance brightness and clarity without sacrificing the integrity of the picture. A more captivating and visually arresting shot is produced when haze is deliberately targeted and eliminated, allowing the underlying colors and textures to come through.

All you have to do is find the Haze removal function in the menu or toolbar and apply it to the relevant picture. With only a few clicks, photographers can easily improve the visual quality of their images thanks to the user-friendly interface that guarantees accessibility.

Auto Color Correction

This command skillfully modifies the color of your picture to provide a more realistic and natural appearance by addressing subtleties in color. It takes off color casts, evens out skin tones, and boosts your image's brightness.

Auto Sharpen

This command introduces a sharpening filter to enhance the edges and details within your image. The outcome is a heightened sense of definition and focus, ensuring that key elements stand out with clarity

Auto Red-Eye Fix

The Red-Eye Removal command is a specific tool for identifying and removing the prevalent red-eye issue caused by flash photography. This specific effect happens when the flash from the camera bounces off the blood vessels in the retina, giving the individuals' eyes a crimson glow. Specifically developed to address this problem and improve the overall quality of portrait images is the Red-Eye Removal command.

Using this command on images with subjects facing the camera directly yields the best results. The gadget detects the telltale red-eye impact and uses intelligence to target and remove undesirable eye discoloration, looking into the eyes a more natural and appealing appearance. The Red-Eye Removal command's algorithm is put to identify common red-eye patterns, providing precise repair.

The Red-Eye Removal function is readily located in the menu or toolbar, allowing for quick and easy use. Photographers can get outcomes that seem professional without having to make a lot of manual modifications because of the user-friendly UI.

Practically speaking, the Red-Eye Removal command improves the overall quality of face characteristics in pictures in addition to resolving the technical issue of red-eye. The tool makes sure that the eyes, which are often regarded as the main point of a photograph, seem clear, lively, and true to their original color by removing annoying red-eye effects.

To leverage these Auto Fixes commands, adhere to the following steps:

1. **Open Image and Access Quick Workspace:** Open your image and navigate to the Quick Workspace.
2. **Invoke Auto Fixes**: Opt for the Auto Fixes button within the Quick Actions panel or choose Enhance > Auto Fixes from the menu bar.
3. **Select Auto Fix Command:** Choose the specific Auto Fix command that aligns with your desired adjustments. Utilize the keyboard shortcuts provided for added efficiency.
4. **Preview and Adjust:** Preview the effects of the Auto Fix command on your image. If necessary, use the Undo button or the Ctrl+Z (Windows) or Command+Z (Mac) shortcut to revert changes before finalizing.
5. **Save or Continue Editing:** Save your image with the applied enhancements or seamlessly transition to other tools and commands for further refinement.

Shifting Image with Content-Aware Move Tool

The Content-Aware Move tool is a powerful feature that empowers users to effortlessly select and relocate a specific portion of an image to a different location. This tool stands out for its automated capability to intelligently fill in the vacated area, seamlessly blending the moved element with the surrounding pixels.

To effectively utilize the Content-Aware Move tool, follow these comprehensive steps:

1. **Select the Content-Aware Move Tool**: Located in the toolbar, identify and select the Content-Aware Move tool. Recognizable by its crosshair appearance with an arrow, this tool is instrumental in precise image manipulation.
2. **Choose the Mode in the Options Bar**: In the options bar, decide on the mode that best suits your editing needs. Opt for the Move mode when relocating an object or select the Extend mode to duplicate an object, providing versatile functionality for a range of creative adjustments.
3. **Create a Selection:** Employ any of the available selection tools, such as the Lasso or Quick Selection tool, to delineate a precise selection around the portion of the image you intend to move or extend. This step ensures accuracy and control in targeting the specific area for manipulation.
4. **Drag and Nudge the Selection:** With the selection made, drag it to the new location where you want to place it. For meticulous adjustments, utilize the arrow keys to nudge the selection incrementally, facilitating fine-tuned positioning.
5. **Apply the Change:** Press Enter or click the green checkmark icon to execute the changes. Photoshop Element will dynamically fill in the gap created by the moved or duplicated part, seamlessly integrating it with the background. The blending process ensures a natural and cohesive result.

CHAPTER THIRTEEN

ADJUSTING IMAGE CONTRAST, SHARPNESS AND COLOR

Adjusting Lighting

In both Quick and Expert modes, the Lighting panel allows users to enhance the visual dynamics of their photos using a comprehensive toolkit. Photographers and designers can finely adjust the lighting qualities of their compositions, including exposure, contrast, highlights, shadows, and whites.

In Quick and Expert modes, the Lighting panel becomes the primary tool for enhancing an image's visual impact. With this versatile toolset, users can customize the lighting to suit each photograph's unique needs and creative vision. The panel provides various options to achieve different objectives, such as highlighting important parts, bringing out subtle details in shadows, and finding the right balance between exposure and contrast. Within this panel, users can adjust contrast for a more dynamic visual effect, highlight and shadows to achieve the ideal balance between light and dark areas, and exposure to control the image's overall brightness. Additionally, the ability to adjust whites allows for enhancing the picture's brightness, contributing to a harmoniously balanced and aesthetically pleasing composition.

The Auto button in the Lighting panel is a time-saving option for those seeking a quick and effective fix. By pressing the Auto button, Photoshop Elements takes over, evaluating the picture and automatically adjusting the lighting for the user. This feature is particularly useful for those who prefer a simplified process or need a starting point before manually adjusting specific details.

The Lighting panel serves as a flexible ally in achieving ideal lighting for every shot, whether working in Quick mode for swift adjustments or exploring the complex possibilities of Expert mode. Its intuitive interface and robust features, combined with a mix of automation and human refining, cater to a range of editing tastes and ability levels, making it an invaluable tool for photographers and designers.

Adjust Lighting with Shadows/Highlights

The Shadows/Highlights feature, found in the enhanced menu bar, provides advanced picture modifications and a powerful toolbox for enhancing highlights and shadows. This command allows users to precisely control the distribution of tones in their photographs, ensuring a pleasing balance of light and shadow.

To utilize the Shadows/Highlights command, users can access it through the menu bar. This function enables the deliberate highlighting of dark areas and regulated highlighting of excessively bright portions within an image. It is particularly useful in challenging lighting conditions or when certain aspects are overly prominent in highlights or concealed in shadows.

Furthermore, the Shadows/Highlights command offers a more sophisticated level of customization than simple lighting adjustments. Users can enhance its impact by modifying the radius, tone, and quantity of the effect. The quantity control allows for subtle or strong alterations to shadow and highlight intensity, while the tone adjustment facilitates changes to color balance in the affected areas, ensuring seamless integration with the overall color scheme of the image. Additionally, the radius control provides the flexibility to choose the extent to which changes are applied across the image, offering a tailored solution for different compositions.

This dynamic command breathes life into photos that may lack vibrancy due to insufficient contrast or uneven lighting. When aiming for a well-balanced and visually appealing outcome, the Photoshop Element Shadows/Highlights command proves to be a valuable tool for bringing out details in darker areas and controlling overly bright highlights.

Adjust Lighting with Brightness/Contrast

The Brightness/Contrast command, found in the enhanced menu bar, is a valuable tool for users seeking to modify the overall brightness and contrast of their photos. Photographers and designers can utilize this command to align the brightness and contrast with their creative vision, providing a straightforward yet effective means of enhancing visual dynamism.

Efficient use of the Brightness/Contrast command involves accessing the Enhance menu, initiating a process that enables users to adjust the brightness and contrast levels of their images. With two functions, this command can be tailored to meet various editing requirements, allowing users to modify the overall brightness and contrast.

An outstanding feature is the Auto button, which streamlines the adjustment process, saving time. By simply pressing Auto, Photoshop Elements can optimize brightness and contrast, offering a quick enhancement or preliminary adjustment before fine-tuning individual elements manually.

Moreover, the utility of the Brightness/Contrast command is further enhanced by enabling users to customize the impact according to their preferences, rather than imposing a universal modification. This flexibility empowers users to achieve the ideal balance between brightness and contrast, whether aiming for a dramatic change or a subtle adjustment.

Adjust Lighting with Levels

The Levels command in the enhance menu bar is a powerful tool for adjusting your image's color balance and tone range. You can precisely specify key factors like the black point, white point, and mid-tone by analyzing the histogram details and adjusting them using the sliders. With this level of control, you can create a visually striking composition with improved tonal dynamics and color balance by carefully adjusting the shadows, highlights, and midtones. By utilizing these capabilities, you can ensure that your picture is finely tuned, resulting in a sophisticated and polished end product.

Adjusting Image Color

The Color panel is a tool that can be used in both Quick and Expert modes. It offers a range of adjustments to enhance the visual appeal of the image. Use this panel to easily modify key elements such as saturation, vibrance, hue, and temperature. By manipulating these factors, you can effectively control the warmth or coolness of your picture, apply a desired tint, increase or decrease the brightness of colors, and adjust overall saturation. As a result, the Color panel serves as a comprehensive hub for creating a dynamic and compelling visual narrative. It allows you to precisely fine-tune the color scheme of your picture in a quick edit or a more detailed one.

Removing Color Casts

A color cast can be described as an undesirable shift in the color balance of a photograph. For instance, a photo captured indoors without the use of a camera flash might exhibit an excess of yellow tones. The Remove Color Cast command becomes an invaluable tool in rectifying such issues by globally adjusting the color mixture, effectively eliminating the unwanted color cast from the image.

To utilize the Remove Color Cast feature, follow these steps:

1. Navigate to Enhance > Adjust Color > Remove Color Cast.
2. In your image, select a portion that is intended to be white, black, or neutral gray. The image dynamically adjusts based on the color you choose.
3. Should you wish to revert the changes and start afresh, click Reset.
4. Finally, confirm the color adjustments by clicking OK.

Adjust Color with Hue Saturation

Use this procedure to precisely optimize your color adjustments non-destructively, go to Enhance > Adjust Color > Adjust Hue/Saturation or choose Layer > New Adjustment Layer > Hue/Saturation to create an adjustment layer.

When you select Colorize, Photoshop Elements cleverly adjusts your picture to match the foreground color while maintaining the pixel-by-pixel brightness values. The program easily adapts to any hue in the foreground that isn't black or white, providing users with a flexible canvas for experimenting with color combinations.

You can further refine your colorization by using the Hue slider, which allows you to manually choose a new color that best fits your artistic

vision. Adjust the saturation of the chosen color by dragging the slider to change its intensity. As you make these changes, observe how your picture is transformed in real-time into something more brilliant.
To confirm the modifications, simply click OK if you're satisfied with the chosen hue and saturation settings. With this approach, you can experiment with different color schemes, giving your graphics a new lease of life with unparalleled freedom and control, all while maintaining a smooth and non-destructive workflow.

Removing Image Color / Converting Color Image to Black and White

To easily eliminate all colors from your image, layer, or designated area, utilize Photoshop Elements' powerful "Remove Color" feature. This single-step function streamlines the color removal process and enhances user-friendliness. Navigate to Enhance→Adjust Color→Remove Color in your Photoshop Elements toolbox to access this capability. This straightforward command enables you to swiftly achieve a monochromatic appearance and enhance your control over the project's visual elements.

Swapping Color with Replace Color Command

The Replace Color dialog in Photoshop is a comprehensive tool that combines color range selection tools with intuitive sliders for adjusting Hue, Saturation, and Lightness, facilitating seamless color replacements. When aiming for a complete color transformation, the dialog provides a streamlined interface for selecting and replacing specific colors. Unlike the Hue/Saturation adjustment, the Replace Color dialog doesn't include the Colorize option, which is crucial for achieving a full-color change. For targeted color modifications, the adjustment layer technique might be more convenient, but the Replace Color dialog excels in global color alterations, particularly when dealing with out-of-gamut colors for print.

To access the Replace Color dialog, navigate to Image > Adjustments > Replace Color.

Upon opening the dialog, you can choose between two preview options:

- **Selection:** Displays a mask in the preview box, with black indicating masked areas and white representing unmasked areas. Semi-transparent mask areas appear as varying levels of gray.
- **Image:** Displays the image in the preview box, recommended for working with magnified images or limited screen space.

To select the colors for replacement, use the Eyedropper tool to pick an area in the image or preview box. The Localized Color Clusters option is useful for selecting similar, contiguous colors, enhancing the accuracy of the mask.

Refine your selection further with the following options:

- **Add To Sample Eyedropper:** Shift-click to add areas to the selection.
- **Subtract From Sample Eyedropper**: Alt-click (Windows) or Option-click (macOS) to remove areas from the selection.
- **Selection Color Swatch:** Open the Color Picker to fine-tune the selection color.

Adjust the slider to control the inclusivity of related colors in the selection. Specify a replacement color using either the sliders or the

Color Picker. Note that you cannot replace pure gray, black, or white with a color, but you can adjust the Lightness setting.

Upon finalizing your adjustments, select OK to apply the changes to your image. Additionally, the Save option allows you to store these settings for future use with other images. This comprehensive tool provides a versatile and efficient way to manage color adjustments within your projects.

Improving Image Color with Color Curve

The color curve serves as a tool for fine-tuning the tonal range and color equilibrium within an image. This versatile tool allows users to enhance the brightness, darkness, contrast, or overall vibrancy of their images. To harness the capabilities of the color curve, follow these comprehensive steps:

1. Initiate the process by opening your desired image in Photoshop Elements. Navigate to the menu and select Enhance > Adjust Color > Adjust Color Curves to unveil the Adjust Color Curves dialog box.
2. Within the dialog box, peruse the "Select a Style" list and opt for a preset that aligns with your editing objectives. Choices such as Increase Contrast, Darken Highlights, or Cross Process are readily available. Alternatively, choose the Custom option to craft a personalized curve.
3. Begin the modification process by dragging the curve to alter the tonal values of the image. The addition of anchor points can be accomplished by clicking on the curve, and their removal can be achieved by dragging them off the curve. Complementary adjustments can be made using the sliders situated below the curve, enabling precise control over highlights, midtones, and shadows.
4. For refining the color balance, explore the RGB menu and select a specific color channel, be it Red, Green, or Blue. Manipulate the curve accordingly to augment or diminish the presence of that particular color in the image. Additionally, utilize the sliders beneath the curve for fine-tuning the color balance to your liking.
5. Having executed the desired modifications, click OK to implement the changes to your image. The comprehensive adjustments made through the color curve will undoubtedly enhance the visual appeal and aesthetic coherence of your photograph.

Correcting Image Skin Tone

Skin tone adjustments in photos are easy with Photoshop Elements. Unsatisfactory skin tones in your subjects may be due to various photographic variables. The "Adjust for Skin Tone" feature in

Photoshop Elements was designed to address this issue and give human skin tones a more aesthetically pleasing and natural appearance.

In Photoshop Elements, skin tone adjustments can be made to an entire layer or a specific selection. For best results, select the skin areas that need adjustment while keeping the rest of the image intact. This can be done using a selection tool.

After making your selection, open the Menu Bar and choose "Enhance| Adjust Color| Adjust Color for Skin Tone..." to start the adjustment process. Then, click on the skin area you wish to modify. Fine-tune the adjustment by clicking repeatedly until you achieve the desired result. With this targeted approach, you can improve skin tones without unnecessarily altering other aspects of your photo, giving you precise control over the final aesthetic outcome.

Use the "Skin" and "Ambient Light" sliders to make further changes. The "Tan" slider makes it easier to add or subtract brown tones, while the "Blush" slider lets you adjust how much red is added or subtracted. To adjust the overall color, experiment with the "Temperature" slider. Move it to the right for a redder tone or to the left for a bluer one. After making the necessary modifications, click "OK" to apply the changes and complete the improved skin tones in your photo.

Defringe Layer

Defringing a layer is a technique designed to eliminate undesirable color fringes or halos that may be present around the edges of a selection. This process enhances the overall quality of composite images, creating smoother and more natural transitions at the edges. Follow these steps to effectively de-fringe a layer:

1. Initiate the process by opening your image in Photoshop Elements and selecting the specific area you wish to de-fringe. Utilize any selection tool available, such as the Quick Selection tool, Lasso tool, or Magic Wand tool.
2. Navigate to Select > Modify > Expand to increase the selection size by a few pixels, ensuring the inclusion of the fringes in the selection.
3. Further, refine the selection by choosing Select > Modify > Feather, feathering the edges by a few pixels to create a seamless transition between the selected and unselected areas.
4. Duplicate the selected area onto a new layer by selecting Layer > New > Layer via Copy. Optionally, rename the new layer, perhaps as "Defringe" for clarity.
5. Access Enhance > Adjust Color > Remove Color to convert the new layer to grayscale, effectively eliminating the color and addressing the fringes.
6. Open the Layer Style dialog box by selecting Layer > Layer Style > Blending Options.
7. In the Blend If section, adjust the white slider of the Underlying Layer to the left until the fringes disappear. For precise control, hold down the Alt key (Option key on Mac) and split the slider into two halves.
8. Confirm and apply the changes by clicking OK.

Sharpening For Improved Focus

Sharpening is a transformative process that enhances the clarity and details of an image, imparting a focused and crisp appearance. Beyond this, sharpening serves to mitigate noise and blur, contributing to overall image refinement. Various methods can be employed for sharpening, including the Sharpen tool, the Unsharp Mask filter, and the High Pass technique.

Follow these general steps to sharpen an image effectively:

1. Begin by opening your image, and duplicate the layer by pressing Ctrl+J (Windows) or Command+J (Mac).
2. Select the duplicate layer and navigate to Filter > Enhance > Unsharp Mask. This action opens a dialog box enabling adjustment of the Amount, Radius, and Threshold settings. The Amount determines the extent of sharpening, the Radius controls the size of the sharpening area, and the Threshold dictates the contrast required for applying sharpening. A suggested starting point is an Amount of 50%, a Radius of 1 pixel, and a Threshold of 0. Preview the effect and make necessary adjustments.
3. Click OK to apply the Unsharp Mask filter. Fine-tune the sharpening effect using the Opacity slider or the Blend Mode menu in the Layers panel. Adjustments such as lowering the opacity or changing the blend mode to Overlay or Soft Light can yield a more subtle effect.
4. If selective sharpening is desired, utilize a layer mask. Click on the Add Layer Mask icon at the bottom of the Layers panel to introduce a white mask to the duplicate layer. White signifies that the sharpening effect is visible throughout the image. To conceal the effect in specific areas, use the Brush tool with a black foreground color. Conversely, to reveal the sharpening effect, set the foreground color to white. Adjust the Brush size, hardness, and opacity for precise control over the masking effect.
5. Once content with the results, save the image as a new file or overwrite the original to preserve the enhanced attributes. This

process ensures that your sharpened image meets the desired visual standards.

Opening Closed Eyes

Initiate the process of addressing closed eyes in your image by selecting the dedicated Eye tool. Within the Tool Options bar, locate and click on the "Open Closed Eyes" button to activate this specialized function.

For an alternative method, navigate to the menu and choose Enhance > Open Closed Eyes. This command streamlines the process, offering an additional avenue to rectify closed eyes in your image.

These steps ensure that you have the necessary tools at your disposal to seamlessly address closed eyes and enhance the overall visual appeal of your photographs in Photoshop Elements.

Colorizing an Image

Adding vibrant colors to your photos is an enjoyable and imaginative process that can significantly enhance the visual appeal of your images. There are two primary methods for colorizing images in this software: the Automatic Colorize feature, which employs Adobe AI to automatically generate colors, and the Manual Colorize feature, allowing you to personally select and apply colors to specific areas of the image. Below are detailed steps for both methods:

Automatic Colorize:

1. Open your desired photo.

2. Navigate to the menu and select Enhance > Colorize Photo, or use the shortcut Option+Command+R (macOS)/Alt+Ctrl+R (Windows).
3. The Colorize Photo workspace will appear, generating a preview of your image.
4. In the panel on the right, four color options will be presented. Choose the one that complements your vision for the photo.
5. Utilize the Before/After toggle to compare the results with the original photo.
6. If satisfied, click OK to apply the changes. To revert to the original photo, click Reset.

Manual Colorize:

1. Open the image you want to colorize.
2. Access Enhance > Colorize Photo from the menu or use the shortcut Option+Command+R (macOS)/Alt+Ctrl+R (Windows).
3. Toggle the switch in the right panel to select Manual Colorize.
4. In the right panel, employ the Quick Selection Tool or Magic Wand Tool to mark the areas where color changes are desired.
5. Click the Droplet tool and place droplets within the selected areas to specify the regions for recoloring. Multiple droplets can be added based on your preferences.
6. Each droplet will display a set of customizable colors in the Color Palette. Choose a droplet and select the desired color from the palette or use the vertical slider in the All Applicable Colors panel.
7. Toggle off the Show Droplets option to preview the result without visible droplets.
8. Use the Before/After toggle to compare the original and edited versions.
9. To discard all changes and revert to the original photo, click Reset.

7. Once content with the outcome, click OK to apply the manual colorization.

The Smooth Skin Feature

The new Smooth Skin function simplifies the process of enhancing the visual appeal of your photos. This tool, powered by advanced Adobe AI technology, effectively reduces wrinkles, blemishes, and imperfections. It offers a convenient solution for enhancing overall appearance.

Activate the Smooth Skin option from the Quick Actions menu and begin experiencing its benefits. You can adjust the strength of the effect to customize its impact, ensuring that your photos maintain their natural look while achieving the desired level of refinement.

But the enhancements don't stop there. Delve deeper into Photoshop Elements creative toolkit with the Color Match feature. This additional function allows you to match the hue and tone of your image to another, creating a cohesive visual narrative that seamlessly connects across your collection.

The capabilities of Photoshop Elements offer a powerful yet user-friendly approach to photo enhancement, whether you're seeking to harmonize color schemes or diminish fine lines. Learn how to maximize your photos by harnessing the potent capabilities of Color Match and Smooth Skin, expertly designed to elevate the visual impact of your images.

Photoshop's Discover Panel can be used to boost your creative pursuits with a variety of tools that are easy to learn and adapt to. Use the search icon in the top right corner of the program workspace to open the Discover Panel. Or use the handy keyboard shortcut Cmd/Ctrl + F, or use the menu bar and choose Help > Photoshop Help.

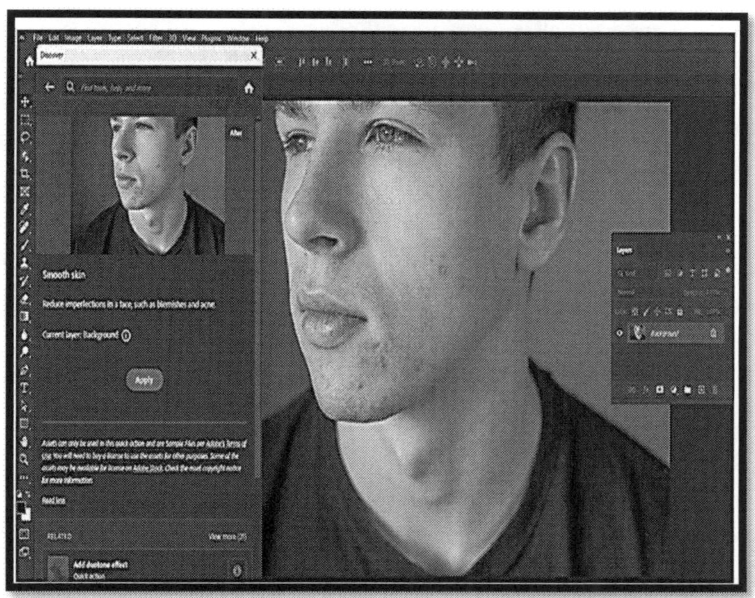

After you're in the Discover Panel, choose Browse > Quick Actions and then click on "Smooth Skin". Click the Apply button to put the improvement into action. You can easily choose the topic of your picture.

There is an extra step needed for first-time users of the Smooth Skin fast action. To get the neural filter required for this fast action, click the Download button. Apply the Smooth Skin enhancer for a more sophisticated and polished appearance after downloading.

Go to the Discover panel > Quick Actions > Smooth Skin, then click Apply to discover other options. Try the action on a different layer for more flexibility by choosing the appropriate layer from the Layers window, and then clicking Refresh to continue.

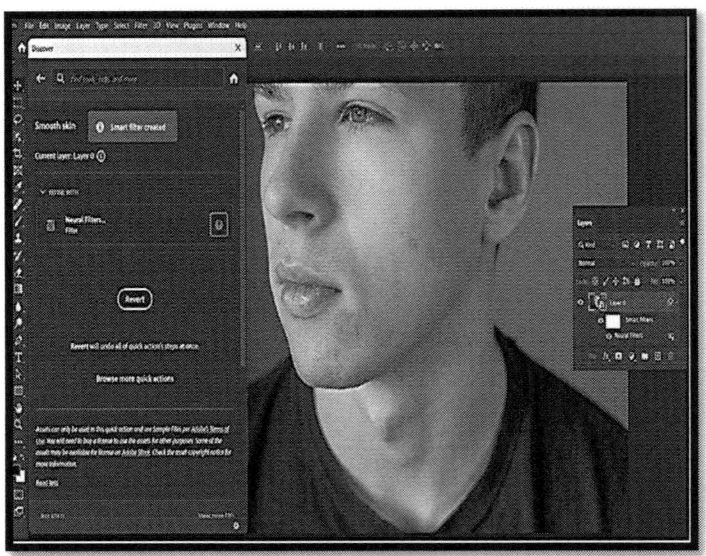

Use the Revert option if you want to reverse any changes that have been made. Click Explore more fast actions to find additional quick actions for your photographs. This will show you a variety of improvements that you can use to make your creative efforts stand out.

Adjusting Facial Features

Face-Aware Liquify is a Photoshop plugin that may be used to improve portraits or add a fanciful touch to humorous photos. It automatically recognizes face characteristics, opening up new creative options.

Here's a step-by-step guide to accentuating a surprised expression in a sample image by manipulating facial features:

1. **Open an Image:** Begin by launching Photoshop and opening an image containing a face. For future flexibility in readjustments, consider converting the layer to a Smart Object by right-clicking or control-clicking before opening in Liquify. Navigate to Filter > Liquify to access the Liquify window.

2. **Enlarge the Eyes:** In the Liquify window, unfold Face-Aware Liquify by clicking the triangle. If there are multiple faces, use the Select Face menu to choose the specific face to adjust. Focus on the eyes by clicking the triangle next to Eyes. Adjust the size, height, width, tilt, and/or distance using sliders. Alternatively, directly click and drag on facial features using the Face Tool in the Toolbar for more intuitive adjustments.

3. **Adjust the Shape of the Nose:** Click the triangle next to the Nose to unveil sliders for shaping the nose. Modify the Nose Height slider to elongate the nose and the Nose Width slider to narrow it.

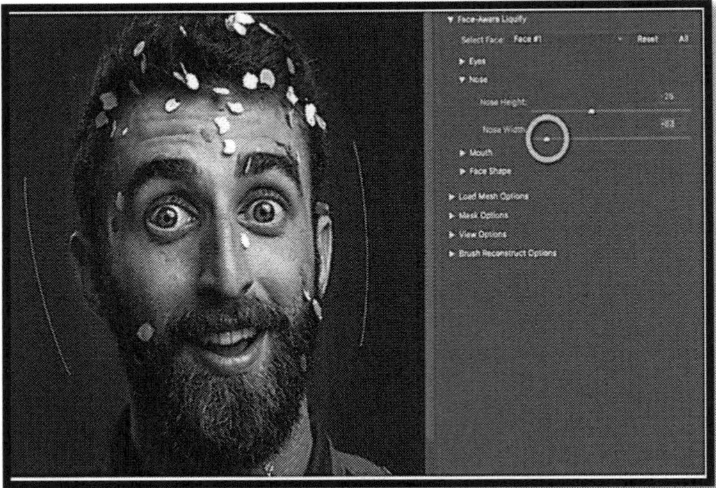

4. **Widen the Smile:** For adjustments to the mouth area, click the triangle next to Mouth. Utilize sliders such as Smile, Lower Lip, Mouth Width, and Mouth Height to customize the smile and lip dimensions.

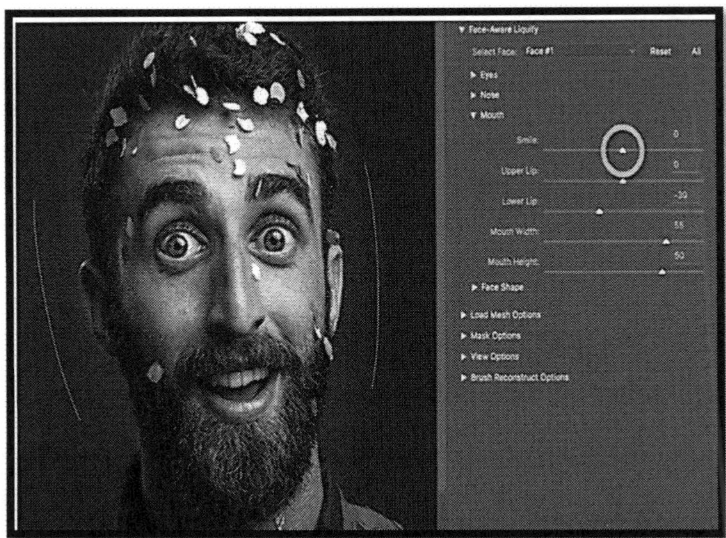

5. **Elongate the Face:** Explore the Face Shape triangle to alter the overall shape. Drag the Forehead Height slider to elongate the forehead, the Jawline slider to expand the jaw, and the Face Width slider to contract the face width.

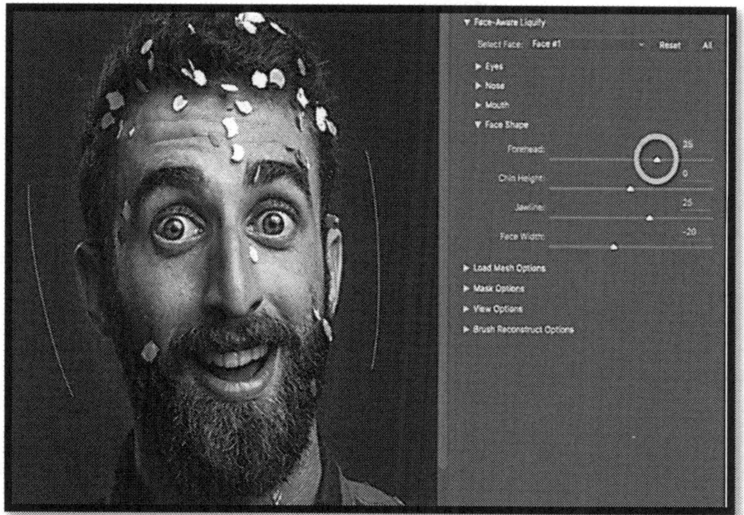

6. **Close Liquify and Save:** Click OK to exit the Liquify window. Save your edited image by selecting File > Save. Embrace the transformed image, showcasing the creative potential of Face-Aware Liquify.

INDEX

Made in the USA
Middletown, DE
04 March 2024